American Men of Letters.

EDITED BY

CHARLES DUDLEY WARNER.

F.T. Stuart

Geo. Ripley

GEORGE RIPLEY,

BY

OCTAVIUS BROOKS FROTHINGHAM.

BOSTON AND NEW YORK

HOUGHTON MIFFLIN COMPANY

𝔗he 𝔕iverside 𝔓ress 𝔠ambridge

3627
PS
2713
F76

CONTENTS.

3627

CHAPTER VIII.

CHAPTER IX.

GEORGE RIPLEY.

CHAPTER I.

EARLY DAYS. — MINISTRY.

THE purpose of this memoir is to recover the image and do justice to the character of a remarkable man, the pursuits of whose latter years gave him little opportunity to display his deepest convictions, while his singular charm of manner and conversation concealed from all but those who knew him well the recesses of his feelings; a man of letters, a man too of ideas and purposes which left a broad mark on his age, and deserve to be gratefully borne in mind.

George Ripley was born in Greenfield, the shire town of Franklin County, Massachusetts, — a fair spot in the Connecticut Valley, about ninety miles west from Boston, — on the third day of October, 1802. He was the youngest but one of ten children, four boys and six girls, all of whom died before him. His brother Franklin, a graduate of Dartmouth College, educated as a lawyer, and for many years cashier of the Greenfield bank, a man of mark, honored and trusted, died in 1860. His dearly beloved sister Marianne, a woman of superior mental

1

gifts, as well as of the highest personal qualities, closely acquainted with many prominent
men and women of her time, an engaging
teacher, and an earnest fellow-worker with her
brother at Brook Farm, died at Madison, Wisconsin, in May, 1868. The father, Jerome Ripley, born in Hingham, moved from Boston to
Greenfield in 1789. He is described by David
Willard, the historian of Greenfield, as a man
" whose integrity was never even suspected ; of
whose virtue and uprightness a long course of
years leaves no question ; an eminent example
of the beneficial effects of steady industry and
perseverance in one calling, and of minding
one's own business." He was a merchant, a
justice of the peace nearly fifty years, a representative in the state Legislature, and one of
the justices of the court of sessions. The
mother, a connection of Benjamin Franklin
(her great-grandfather was Dr. Franklin's uncle), was a good example of a New England
woman, frugal, precise, formal, stately, reserved,
but kind and warm-hearted at the core. She
was Orthodox in religion ; her husband was
Unitarian. There was then in Greenfield, a
town of about fifteen hundred inhabitants, but
one church ; the Second Congregational society
having been formed in 1816, the Third, or Unitarian, in 1825. At the ordination there, in

1837, of John Parkman, George Ripley took part.

In 1831 Ezra Stiles Gannett, returning from a visit to Greenfield, writes: " I have always found my mind, after a visit to this place or Connecticut, in a very different state from what is usual at home. My thoughts are more directed to the subject of religion, of vital and internal piety. Conference and religious meetings are common, and religion seems more an every-day thing than with us." Six years later, in 1837, Theodore Parker went there. The place was charming, but the parish was not attractive. The meetings were held in a courtroom. There were five societies for less than two thousand people. The sectarian activity was greatly in excess of the spiritual. The centres of thought were distant; the weekly mail from Boston came on horseback. George Ripley had pleasant memories of his early life in this delightful region. A little more than a year before his death he affectionately recalled scenes, persons, and social features of that " primitive, beautiful country life," but he went there seldom, as his thoughts were engrossed by larger concerns.

He began his education at the public school, a good one. In 1838 there were seven, showing a remarkable interest in education for so

small a community. The only reminiscence of
his early mental habits is a frequently expressed
desire to " make a dictionary," a curious an-
ticipation of his future employment. At Cambridge he was known as a remarkably handsome
youth, with bright piercing eyes, an excellent
scholar, especially in the languages and in literature; he excelled also in the mathematics,
which afterwards, during part of his stay in
Cambridge, as a student of theology, he taught
in his college. Twice he received the second
Bowdoin prize.

HADLEY, *June* 16, 1818.

MY DEAR MOTHER, — . . . We have a very large
school this term, about one hundred and thirty. Mr.
Huntingdon calculates to fit me for college before
next Commencement. I suspect that if my health is
good I can read the Testament and Minora this
term, which is all that is required at Yale. **To fail
is** absolutely impossible. In haste,

GEORGE RIPLEY.

HADLEY, *July* 10, 1818.

HONORED PARENT, — . . . This quarter expires
on the 11th of August, about six weeks from this
time. I expect then to have studied the Minora and
arithmetic. There will then be only a fortnight before Commencement, and the remaining studies which
I need are the Greek Testament and algebra and

ancient and modern geography. You will easily perceive that it will be impossible for me to become acquainted with these before the term commences. I may perhaps, with hard study and previous calculations, by a year from next fall be fitted as a Sophomore, if you should conclude to send me to Cambridge. The Commencement at Yale is the second week in September, with a vacation of six weeks. All that I shall be deficient in at the end of the quarter, of the preparatory studies required at Yale, will be the Greek Testament. A knowledge of that I could easily obtain, and before the commencement of the term be well fitted and enabled to have a respectable standing in the class. I think it is altogether necessary for me to know what arrangements are made respecting me, before the expiration of this term. I feel grateful that you are willing to be at the additional expense of educating me, and I hope that I shall duly appreciate the favor. It shall be my endeavor, by economy and self-denial, to render the burden as light as possible. But I feel emboldened to make the request that, if consistent with your inclinations and plans, I may receive an education at Yale rather than Cambridge. I may be thought assuming and even impertinent to make this request. But, sir, I entreat you to consider the thing. The literary advantages at Cambridge are superior in some respects to those at Yale. The languages can undoubtedly be learnt best at Cambridge. But it is allowed by many, who have had opportunity to judge, free from prejudice, that the solid branches may be acquired to as great perfection at Yale. Cousin Henry, who has had some information on the subject, says that for mathematics, metaphysics, and for the solid sciences in general, Yale is the best. The temptations incident to a college, we have reason to think, are less at Yale than at Cambridge.

I remain your obliged and affectionate son,

GEORGE RIPLEY.

WALTHAM, *June* 12, 1819.

MY DEAR MOTHER, — We had upon the whole a pleasant journey, though it was rendered disagreeable by the extreme heat and dust and the number of passengers. We arrived at Lincoln about eight in the evening, where we met Dr. Ripley, who carried us to Concord. There I passed the night and part of the next day, and in the afternoon rode to Waltham with cousin Sarah. She stated the case to Mr. Ripley, who was willing to instruct me, and after an examination expressed his opinion that probably I might enter at Cambridge, if not at Commencement, at the close of the vacation. He has a house full of boys, two of whom are to be examined in the fall. The advantages here for being well prepared for college are indeed many. His system of instruction is altogether different from anything which I have been accustomed to. It is pretty certain if I had not come here, or to some other similar place, I should not have been fitted for Cambridge this year ; and as I now am I consider it something doubtful whether I can get in. My boarding-place is at a Mrs. Smith's a very respectable family. The board is $3.00 a week, — a large sum. But I trust that eventually it will be cheaper for me than if I had remained at Greenfield. The place is very pleasant, many beautiful walks and prospects, and a good situation for acquiring knowledge, but the religious state of the place is far different from that of Greenfield.

CAMBRIDGE, *October*, 1819.

DEAR MOTHER, — At length I have got pretty comfortably established in this seminary, and begin to feel at home. I have had a very confused time hitherto, owing to the perplexities and inconveniences which usually attend a student on his first entrance on a collegiate course ; but I now find considerable quiet and tranquillity, and can behold a prospect of profit and improvement. I arrived in Boston the day after leaving Greenfield, and found our friends in health. You probably desire to know concerning my situation and prosperity at this place, but I hardly know what opinion to form myself. As I observed before, the prospect for improvement in learning is favorable. Undoubtedly there are means and privileges here particularly great, such as are enjoyed by no other American college. The course of studies adopted here, in the opinion of competent judges, is singularly calculated to form scholars, and, moreover, correct and accurate scholars ; to inure the mind to profound thought and habits of investigation and reasoning. I am in great hopes that my health wil. be able to endure the exertions necessary to be made

I am not obliged to study at all hard to perform the exercises allotted me.   At present our lessons can all be learnt in three, or at most four, hours.   But the diligent student will find something to occupy all his time, and leave not a moment to be spent in idleness. I expect to have some time to read, and if a judicious choice of books is made it may be profitable.   The expense here will probably be nearly as you expected. The commons are charged according to the price of provisions; but usually there is an extra expense, called *sizing;* that is, if you don't have bread, or butter, or meat, etc., sufficient, you can call for more, and be charged four cents a time.   This amounts, when it is done no oftener than is absolutely necessary, to, say, $2.00 a term.   The books used in the classes are furnished by the University booksellers, at a discount of twenty per cent., to be charged in the quarter bill.   Many second-hand are to be obtained, however, for a trifle.   I bought a very good book, the price of which is $2.80, for two shillings, and one or two others in the same proportion.   My washing I have done at $5.00 per term.

Your affectionate son,   G. RIPLEY.

CAMBRIDGE, HARVARD UNIVERSITY,
November 10, 1819.

MY DEAR MOTHER, — . . . I would say a few words concerning my teaching a school the ensuing winter.   I have no one in particular in view at present, and it may be doubtful whether I can obtain a good one.   If it should be thought expedient, I should be willing to teach one in the vicinity of Greenfield. If I could obtain one in Shelburne, beginning the Monday after Thanksgiving, and continue two months, at the rate of $16.00 a month, it would perhaps be an object. I consider it my duty to use what exertions are in my power to render the burden necessary to complete my education as small as possible. Your affectionate son,

GEORGE RIPLEY.

April 20, 1820.

. . . The commons have deteriorated very much ...is term, and are almost abandoned by the scholars, among the rest by me. I can board at the same price as the commons will be in the bill, and on much more wholesome provisions. I presume you will approve of my change. Next term I hope to board in my room at $2.00, as nearly one fourth of the scholars do. This custom is recently introduced by Professor Everett, who sets the example in imitation of the German universities, whose manners and customs they endeavor to adopt as much as possible.

HARVARD UNIVERSITY, CAMBRIDGE, *May* 15.

MY DEAR MOTHER, — . . . We have been subjected to many temporary inconveniences for our attachment to what we considered our duty, and what our own interest and the interests of the college demanded. But good has been educed from evil. The division has been so deeply rooted, and animosities are so malignant and inveterate, as effectually to pre

vent much of the social intercourse for which, when
Freshmen, we were particularly distinguished. The
competition for scholarship has been zealous and energetic, and each party jealous of the other strives to
win the prize.

It has been reported by our enemies that the only
object of those who opposed the rebellion was to
secure the favor of the government, and thereby obtain higher college honors. Now it happens that
most of our number are good scholars, and they have
endeavored to prove, and have probably succeeded,
that if they do receive high honors it will be due to
their literary merit, and not to their conduct in this
affair. Mr. Dorr, of whom you have heard me speak,
is one of the most efficient and worthy members of
our party, and is considered by the class as decidedly
the first scholar. He, indeed, possesses a powerful
mind, and has every faculty of appearing to the best
advantage. The tutors say he is the best scholar of
his age they ever knew. He will probably spend
some years in Germany after he leaves Cambridge,
and if his health is spared return one of the most
eminent among our literary men. I am happy to
consider this man my friend, for the excellences of
his heart are not surpassed by the strength of his
genius. I look forward with pleasure, though not
unmingled with regret, to the close of the first half
of my college life. I never expect to be in a state
where I can have superior means of improvement and
happiness; but the minds of young men, inexperienced and ardent, long for emancipation from the re

straints of college and power, to take a more active and more conspicuous part in the great theatre of life. Be it my lot to retire to some peaceful village, where, " the world forgetting, and by the world forgot," I may pass the remainder of my days in study and labor. I love sometimes to anticipate such a station as this. Where the Lord will appoint the bounds of my habitation I cannot see. My duty, however, at present is plain : diligently to improve the advantages I enjoy, aspire after high intellectual and moral and religious excellence, and do what I can for the good of those around me.

CAMBRIDGE, HARVARD UNIVERSITY,
April 6, 1821.

MY DEAR MARIANNE, — . . . The dull monotony of college life presents little that is interesting to strangers, and the confinement to abstruse studies chills the ardor of feeling which is so necessary to the cultivation of the more kindly and tender affections. Notwithstanding, I hope that I shall be able to maintain a more intimate and regular intercourse with my much-loved home. Our studies are so altered this term as to allow more time for our own concerns ; but they are still severe, and, if faithfully attended to, will occupy most of our time and thoughts. The path of knowledge is difficult and embarrassing, requiring the highest exertions of all our faculties. But it is a cause in which we richly receive the reward of our labors. The prospect of devoting my days to the acquisition and communication of knowl ledge is bright and cheering ; this employment I would not exchange for the most elevated station of wealth or honor.   One of the happiest steps, I think, that I have ever taken was the commencement of a course of study, and it is my wish and effort that my future progress may give substantial evidence of it. It is interesting to contemplate the characters of great and good men of other times, and trace the path by which they arrived at excellence.   We see much, however, in many of the most eminent men which cannot command our approbation, and frequently that awakens our disgust.   In a religious view, perhaps, the greatest part of those whose names are conspicu- ous on the records of fame deserve reprobation.   We shall see that they were actuated by motives of a worldly and selfish ambition, and their very virtues were so mingled with what is evidently corrupt that we are in doubt whether they deserve that name. There is, indeed, a deceitful splendor cast around them by the art of the historian, but this very cir cumstance is suited to misguide and delude the youth· ful mind.   There is great danger lest, in the inexpe- rienced and sanguine season of youth, we acquire admiration of those characters, and adopt them as models, which cannot fail to be productive of the most injurious consequences.   But there are some whom we can safely imitate.   Such was Cowper. " His virtues formed the magic of his song."   Of this class was Dr. Dwight.   I have never read of any one, I think, who approached nearer to perfection of character. . . .

I send up Dr. Channing's lecture, supposing my father would like to have it; and, by the way, mention that he is the author of the very beautiful memoir of Gallison in the last "Christian Disciple."

Yours, affectionately,   G. RIPLEY.

HARVARD UNIVERSITY, *July* 12, 1821.

MY DEAR MARIANNE, — . . . I long to see you all; and though you know I have no enthusiastic attachment to Greenfield, I would gladly transport myself thither this moment, to enjoy a few days in the good old hospitable, beautiful mansion. After six weeks of hard digging, I hope to partake of that happiness. Our studies, however, though hard, are singularly pleasant. We have made some progress in the intricate mazes of metaphysics, but, with such a guide as our learned Professor Hedge, we find our difficulties much lessened. We are now studying Locke, an author who has done more to form the mind to habits of accurate reasoning and sound thought than almost any other.

HARVARD UNIVERSITY *July* 17, 1821.

. . . If ever I get through this Sophomore year, I hope to have some few occasional moments, at least, to devote to what I choose. Now that is out of the question; the class are rapidly going on, and unless I give myself to their studies I shall forever lose the important knowledge. . . . Last Tuesday the Senior class had their valedictory exercises. It was a class always distinguished for unanimity, and the parting scene could not be otherwise than solemn and affecting. More tears were shed than ever I witnessed, or had an idea of, among a company of men. This class contains some young men of the highest promise. The Commencement will probably be the best there has been here for years.

Affectionately your son,   GEORGE.

HARVARD UNIVERSITY, *October* 30, 1822.

MY DEAR MOTHER, — . . . I have engaged a school in Fitchburg, expecting to raise about $40.00. This is certainly better than being devoured by indolence and *ennui* in a long vacation. It begins immediately after Thanksgiving, and if the wagoner does not come twice before then, the next time I shall wish to have him bring sundry little conveniences. Yours, affectionately,   G. R.

FITCHBURG, *December* 14, 1822.

MY DEAR MOTHER, — It is now a week since I became an inmate in the family of a good, honest, homespun farmer, and assumed the highly important and respectable office of instructing some forty overgrown, dirty, mischief-loving boys in the mysteries of the spelling-book and Adams's arithmetic. I have deferred writing until this time for several reasons. I had not become acquainted with the regulations of the mail, etc. I live at some distance from anybody but my "parishioners," who are not of that class who form the Corinthian columns of society; and above all, I find that head and hands and eyes and tongue

have their full quota of employment in superintend-
ing the economy of my little empire. This is Saturday afternoon, equally grateful, I presume, to the
scholars and to "the master," as I am universally
called. My situation, although one in which I shall
be but a short time, I suppose you wish to be acquainted with. I cannot, however, give you a precise idea of it. It is a school in the outskirts of this
town, where nature appears in all its loneliness and
wildness, if not magnificence and loveliness. And it
is, upon the whole, a very pleasant school. The
scholars have been under good instruction, and are
singularly attentive to their studies. I have six or
seven great boys, much larger than myself, who study
surveying, chemistry, philosophy, etc., so that there
is some scope for the exercise of intellect. Most of
them are studying grammar, geography, and arithmetic. I am determined to exert myself and keep a
good school. I can certainly, I think, make myself
useful here. There is no particular society in my
district, but in the middle of the town, two miles off,
there are some families whom I shall visit occasionally with pleasure. I could give you a most curious
account of the customs, etc., but it might not be exactly prudent. Suffice it to say, I see human nature
under forms that I had scarcely dreamed of ; still,
I get information from it, and there is no knowledge
but what is valuable. Three years ago I should have
been miserably homesick at such a place, but I have
learned to shape myself to circumstances. I conform
entirely to the manners of the people, and drink cider

and tell stories about cattle with as much grace as ever I figured among the literati at Cambridge. You would hardly know me, with a long beard and dirty shirt, and the worst clothes I can find. So much for Fitchburg. I spent Thanksgiving at Concord, and had a good time.

May 2, Friday Evening.

MY DEAR MOTHER, — . . . Five of our class were expelled to-day, Robinson among them. The class — that is to say, of course, all but the friends of order — are in a state of infuriated excitement and rebellion. What will take place to-morrow I will not venture to predict. It will not surprise us if all the class are cut off down to those who have uniformly proved themselves the supporters of good discipline. It may be that the whole of us will be ordered to leave Cambridge ; in that case I shall of course come home. If not, in the present exigency it will be impossible to quit. In haste yours,

GEORGE RIPLEY.

May 3, 1823.

MY DEAR MOTHER, — . . . In consequence of the expulsion of four who were distinguished in the attack, the class, or a considerable portion rather, re-belled, and they are all gone. Those who remain are sober men of both parties. As regards myself, I am so fortunate as to have escaped any censure from the government of the class. True to my old prin-ciples, of course, I did not join the mob, and have en-teavored to keep myself quiet. . . .

HARVARD UNIVERSITY, *June*, 1823.

MY DEAR FATHER, — As I have never had the opportunity of conversing particularly with you on the course proper for me to adopt on the termination of my connection with the college, I take the liberty of expressing my own views and of requesting your advice. If I were governed merely by the hope of success in life, and perhaps of some degree of eminence, I should by all means endeavor to perfect my education by an elaborate course of study, and a resolution to avoid all thoughts of engaging in the duties of a profession till after a laborious preparation of many years. This plan I am advised to adopt by some in whose judgment I should place high confidence. And were I possessed of a moderate fortune, I believe that inclination and duty would both prompt me to this enterprise, as laying the broadest foundation for future usefulness. The idea of a foreign university would perhaps appear visionary, and in my case I will confess it is entirely so. Still I cannot avoid all regret at beholding the superior advantages which are accessible to our fortunate young men, and wishing myself able to enjoy them. For I know that my peculiar habits of mind, imperfect as they are, strongly impel me to the path of active intellectual effort; and if I am to be at any time of any use to society, or a satisfaction to myself or my friends, it will be in the way of some retired literary situation, where a fondness for study and a knowledge of books will be more requisite than the busy, calculating mind of a man in the business part of the community. I do not mean to say by this that any profession is desired but the one to which I have been long looking. My wish is only to enter that profession with all the enlargement of mind and extent of information which the best institution can afford. In my present circumstances, I cannot reasonably hope for anything more than a sedulous effort to avail myself of what the literary resources we have can give. I wish to study my profession thoroughly. I do not feel prepared to enter upon these important inquiries before a more accurate acquaintance is obtained with some subsidiary branches. For this purpose I wish to spend a year at Cambridge, in a course of study which I have prescribed for myself, unconnected with any department in the university. I should prefer to pursue my theological studies at Andover, both because I am convinced that the opportunities for close investigation of the Scriptures are superior there to those at Cambridge, and the spirit of the place, much relaxed from its former severe and gloomy bigotry, is more favorable to a tone of decided piety. This is my present opinion of Andover. I might, after more extensive acquaintance, have reason to alter it. The only objection attending this plan is the expense. . . .

I am your affectionate son,

GEORGE RIPLEY.

July 18, 1823.

MY DEAR MOTHER, — I have the pleasure of informing you that our college course is at length fin

ished, and I may add, with joy. On Tuesday we r
ceived the valedictory from the president, and took on
leave of the college officers at the president's house.
The world is now before us, and our future character depends much on the course we now adopt. I
feel a strong and affectionate attachment to the college and its governors. I have found here my best
friends, and I have been enabled to acquire their confidence. I wish now to devote myself to the cause
of truth and virtue, in the study of a pure religion
and the cultivation of a sound literature. I regret
that I have been unsuccessful hitherto in my attempt
to procure a school. I shall still look out for a suitable one, and may perhaps attain my object. I must
stay here, at any rate, until I have prepared for Commencement, for which occasion I feel very unable to
meet my duty. It affects my spirits materially. The
scale has preponderated in my favor. I have the
first part, and of course an unusual degree of re-
sponsibleness. I am also the author, as you may
have seen in the paper, of a successful Dissertation
for the Bowdoin Prize. . . .

In 1823 he was graduated at Harvard, first
scholar in a class which could boast of William
P. Lunt, Samuel H. Stearns, and Thomas W.
Dorr, of Rhode Island fame. John P. Robinson, the hero of J. R. Lowell's celebrated
rhyme, pressed him hard, but was suspended
from college for the share he took in the " rebellion," and lost his degree, which was given

him in 1845. At the exercises of graduation
Ripley spoke the English oration, the subject
being " Genius as affected by Moral Feeling."
The three years following were spent in the
study of divinity, during a portion of which
he was a member of the College Faculty, rep-
resenting the departments of Mathematics and
Natural Philosophy. Of his life in the Divinity School there is scanty record; but so high
was his rank as a scholar that at the close
of his studies there was throughout academic
circles the expectation for him of a brilliant
future.

CAMBRIDGE, September 30, 1823.

MY DEAR MOTHER, — With pleasure I begin the
labors of my new situation by informing you of my
condition and prospects ; and I know that you will
rejoice with me in the goodness of Providence which
has appointed the bounds of my habitation where I
have every facility for *real improvement.*

The prospects of our Theological School are so
good, and the call in society for a faithful and devoted clergy, who combine liberal views with deep
piety, is daily becoming so urgent, that I cannot regret having chosen this place as the scene of my
theological investigations. Indeed, it is thought by
many competent judges, and among them Dr. Channing, that this institutio.\ presents advantages for
forming *useful, practical* clergymen not inferior to
the foreign universities. He advises William Emer

son to study at Cambridge rather than at Göttingen, believing that though Germany affords the greatest advantages as far as mere literature is concerned, yet that the best education for a minister in New England, taking into account the moral influence and religious feeling, can be obtained at Cambridge. . . . I am remarkably pleasantly situated, and have everything to my mind. My room is in a brick house, — the south end, — the very last house on the right hand of the street in which the printing-office is. I hope that father will have no difficulty in finding it. It is on the lower floor, about as large as our front room, with two recesses in it; these I have divided off by a curtain from the main room, so as to form closets. I have all Mr. Lincoln's books at my disposal, which, together with the few that I own myself, form a very pretty little library. I feel perfectly satisfied that I have acted according to the will of Providence, as far as I can ascertain it, in uniting myself to this school, and that so far from departing from my religious principles, as some would suppose, I have done that which will tend to their improvement and perfection. I could say much on the emotions which are awakened on commencing those studies to which I have long been looking with fond anxiety and earnest hope. I feel that it is solemn indeed to take any step towards an office involving such responsibility, such infinite consequences. But God will use such instruments as He chooses to promote nis truth in the world. . .

CAMBRIDGE, *October* 1, 1823.

MY DEAR MOTHER, — . . . My cares are now
for my books. My walks of pleasure are exchanged
for walks of exercise and health ; and Green River
Bridge has given way to Mr. Norton's study and the
library. And I am glad. Much as I love company
and gayety, I do love study and retirement best ; and
for this reason, when I once get to Cambridge, I feel
that I never wish to go out of it. It would be so, I
suppose, in any place where I had such cherished intellectual friends, and where scarce anything is destitute of associated circumstances, interesting, and to
literary effort and to moral sentiment inspiring. It
may be superstition, but I cannot help the feeling
I have a strong reverence for the Genius of Place,
and to me there is no place for the exercise of free,
vigorous, effectual thought like this ; and after these
remarks you will not ask me why I like Cambridge
so much.

CAMBRIDGE, *October* 14, 1823.

MY DEAR MOTHER, — . . . I am on very different grounds from what I was when an under-graduate.
Then I was led on by others ; now I am left to my
own keeping, and you may judge the weight of responsibility which I must feel. We have exercises
in the Hebrew language three times a week, and once
a week we present the results of our theological reading and investigations on topics pointed out to us by
Dr. Ware. I am besides diligently engaged in Greek
and other subsidiary studies ; so that my time is more
completely and regularly occupied than ever. I hope

to make all these attainments subservient to the great cause of truth. I am much disappointed in what I have learned of the religious character of the school, I confess. I had some prejudices against many of its members, who, destitute of the austerity, I had thought to be deficient in the spirit, of religion. But if a more intimate acquaintance has enabled me to judge rightly, the depth and purity of their religious feeling and the holy simplicity of their lives is enough to humble and shame those who have been long professors of Christianity, and had pretended to superior sanctity. We meet morning and evening for devotional exercises, and I have no hesitation in saying that if I have ever witnessed the display of spirituality and seriousness of devotion it is in these little meetings. . . .

CAMBRIDGE, *November* 3, 1823.

MY DEAR MOLLY, — . . . I am here engaged in a great work, while at home with you I am idle, useless, and unimproving. I have commenced the most interesting studies, which, to me, are superior to anything which can occupy my mind. My business is now well arranged; every hour has its duty, and every day I can look back and most generally "report progress." I am now employed something in the way in which I trust I am destined to pass my life; and if the profession I have chosen is in any degree as rich in sources of delight as the study of it, my lot is indeed a happy one. I expect to pass a life of poverty, and I care not if of obscurity; but give me my Bible and the studies which relate to its interpretation, give me that philosophy which explains our moral faculty and intellect, and I ask not for wealth or fame. I can be useful to my fellow-men. I wish to say a word with regard to the caution you give me concerning a change of sentiments. In the first place, the opinion of the world is but a puff of empty air. Let the world say what it pleases; truth, and truth unpopular and odious, — aye, and that which is stigmatized as heresy and sin, — must be sought and professed by the consistent Christian. . . .

Yours, dear Molly, truly,   GEORGE.

' CAMBRIDGE.

. . . My health has been capital ever since my return. I have entirely escaped the prevailing influenza. We have quite study enough to afford agreeable excitement without being too much to oppress with its burden. The walking is now very fine, and I spend much time in exercise in the open air. I have been in Boston but little since my return, and, with the exception of a very few friends, I have visited but little in Cambridge. I am now writing my second sermon, which I shall preach before the school on Saturday, with the hope that I shall be more successful than I was at first.

MY DEAR MOLLY, — . . . Did you ever see a mill-horse? Such are we, groaning under Hebrew, Biblical Criticism, Polemics, and Metaphysics, — one hard round. No time for the delights of vacation, though I have been to one party at Stephen Higgin

son's, Esq., merely out of honor to the Theological
School, where I saw the incomparable Miss ——,
who unfortunately wears a crutch ; and the learned
Miss ——, whom they call the Immortal, is here. Do
you read the " Christian Register " ? I forget whether
the Doctor takes it or not. I wish to ask if you have
noticed in the two or three last ones some pieces
signed " C." There is a very grave and philosophical
old gentleman, whom I believe you know, but whose
name I would not mention for the world, who has
undertaken to enlighten the good readers of that paper. I hope you will be far from supposing that
his gray wig conceals a curly pate, or his sage and
sombre reflections a light heart and merry spirit.
But the old fellow is sincere. He desired to do good,
and he thought it might be best done by giving some
adventitious dignity to the source from which his
weighty remarks proceed. It is, moreover, amusing
to hear, as this gray-beard walks unseen through our
ample halls, and even makes one of our family, his
merits discussed, and the question gravely asked if
it is not probable that C. means Dr. Channing. But
my time is out. If I have told you any secret, which
I have not, or given your conjectures any food, which
I have, pray be exhorted to keep them to yourself.

And now I conclude my epistle by beseeching
you, lady, to defend me against the righteous indignation of the Doctor at my unhallowed levity and my
still more prancing, undignified, execrable handwriting. Scatter my benedictions. Most truly,

G

. . . After Mr. Young's ordination, at the New South, I shall make strenuous endeavors to spend the vacation at Greenfield. The president told me the other day, as I suggested in my letter to father, that he might wish me to write for him, but I shall not be easily prevented from spending a part, at least, of my vacation at Greenfield. I do not like the idea of spending a long time without study, as every moment in my present situation is precious. I am not one of those who can write or speak from the inspiration of genius, but all that I do must be the result of my own personal untiring efforts. If I am to be useful as a Christian minister, which is the great object of my present ambition, it is by laying a solid foundation of deep, critical, theological knowledge, rather than by any attempts at popular eloquence or fine writing. With these views, you cannot wish me to sacrifice my *improvement* to my *pleasure,* or even to your gratification. . . .

I am ever your affectionate son,

GEORGE R.

CAMBRIDGE, *February* 5, 1824.

DEAR MARY, — I had a very cold ride from Concord, and arrived just at dark. Nothing interesting has occurred to diversify the sameness of our routine. We go on from day to day, — sleep long and eat temperately, cut jokes and characters in the same breath, read the newspapers, and talk about Amherst College and the Greeks and the next President and the levees at Washington. Some books we read, and many title-pages; we study and understand some speculations in philosophy, and dispute about more. There is a fine fund of knowledge floating about in the atmosphere, and in minds which have anything like a chemical affinity for it it lodges; other minds it poisons, and makes them pedantic and proud. I am plodding on very leisurely and very stupidly trying to know a little of everything, and a great deal about Theology and Metaphysics, and eke a bird's-eye view of History; taking care, you may be sure, to solace the interval with sundry vanities in the form of poetry, books, and novels. I went, moreover, last night, to what they call here a select Cambridge party at Miss ——'s, where I talked to the ladies and ate jellies; "in sic creature comforts," you know, I delight. After all, such concerns are about as interesting to me as the "crackling of thorns;" but we cannot always have substantial hickory, nor yet mountain oak, and when the thorns blaze merrily I would not refuse to enjoy the brightness, and especially I would not throw myself upon the tiny fire, like a great green log, to quench the flame which can burn but a little hour at best. So I laughed with the gay and sported with the trifling till almost eleven o'clock, and came home and turned myself to a dry discussion on the value of Intellectual Philosophy with a clear mind and light heart. So much for my dissipation.

You asked me to say something about the article in the "Disciple." For myself, I freely confess that I think it a useful thing and correct. The rigor of my orthodoxy, which is commonly pretty suscepti-

ble, was not offended. Now, if you have any objections which you can accurately and definitely state,
no doubt there is something in it which had escaped
my notice. If your dislike is only a misty, uncertain
feeling about something, you know not what, it were
well to get fairly rid of it by the best means. I am
far from having any sympathy with the writer of the
article, or the school of divines to which he belongs.
I believe his views of religion are quite different
from Dr. Channing's, whom I place first in the list of
Unitarian ministers, and from those clergymen who
enter more deeply into the views entertained by Dr.
C. and Buckminster, Thatcher, Mr. Frisbie, etc. I
do not allude to speculative opinions, but to sentiments connected more with personal, experimental
religion. But this topic I must reserve till I see you,
and am yours ever,   G. R.

CAMBRIDGE, *July* 18, 1824.

MY DEAR SISTER, — . . . I wish I could give
you an idea of the solemnities at Mr. Gannett's ordination, but a description on paper would be so flat
and inadequate that I will not attempt it. It was a
day of great joy for those who wish to see fervent
piety connected with sound doctrine and liberal feel
ings. I would, but I cannot, enable you to form a
conception of the infantine simplicity and apostolic
meekness, united with the eloquence of an angel and
spirituality of a sainted mind, which characterize Dr.
Channing. His sermon will be printed.

I send you up Locke's Botany, though I doub

whether you will find the grapes of Eshcol or the rose of Sharon in your botanical studies. I would give much more for the fragrance and richness of a cultivated flower than for an accurate knowledge of the stamens and petals and pistils of all the wild flowers on our western mountains. . . .

Yours,   G RIPLEY.

HARVARD UNIVERSITY, *November 24th.*

MY DEAR MOTHER, — . . . I believe the more judicious we become, the less confidence we shall place in some appendage of religion, and the more charity we shall have for others, although we may think widely different from them. In short, true religion is in the heart, and is not connected with any form or any language. . . .

CAMBRIDGE, *December 10, 1824.*

MY DEAR MOTHER, — . . . I returned yesterday from Salem, where I had been attending Mr. Upham's ordination. I can give you no adequate idea of the pleasure of the visit. I would describe the great interest of the occasion, the deep feeling of the society, the enthusiasm excited by the recollections connected with this venerable church, — the first one established in New England by our Pilgrim Fathers, — the contrast of the present situation with that of the great and good men who, when they had built seven houses in Naumkeag, — for so the Indians called what is now Salem, — erected an eighth, and consecrated it to the worship of Almighty God,

— these associations I would describe; but it requires more eloquence than I possess to do them justice.

Mr. Upham's prospects of a happy, useful, and respectable ministry are indeed brilliant. It is a very religious, intelligent people to whom he ministers. They have been early educated in the fear of God, and as a society beautifully display the pure and lovely fruits of our divine faith. They appear very much to act up to the spirit of the exhortation, "Beloved, let us love one another, for love is of God, and he that dwelleth in love dwelleth in God and He in him." There have been some unhappy divisions in the society, but they have terminated in the peace and harmony of the First Church. I went to Salem with Upham on Tuesday, who introduced me to the family of one of his most respectable parishioners, Judge White, where I soon found myself quite at home, and where I stayed with Upham and Mrs. Holmes and several intelligent gentlemen till Thursday. I was glad to form several acquaintances here with distinguished individuals whom I had long known as public men, but not as private persons: for instance, the venerable Timothy Pickering, whom I suppose my father reveres as the apostle of Federalism, — a most delightful old man, with all the simplicity and modesty of a child; John Pickering, the best Greek scholar in New England; Dr. Bowditch; and last, not least, Dr. Channing, whom I never before met. I say nothing of several merchants, who a good deal interested me by their liberality and wide views and charming manners, for were I to particularly men

tion them I could not tell when to begin or when to
stop. The religious exercises were solemn and impressive, — especially the prayers of Drs. Channing
and Sewell, which were enough to excite devotion
in a heart of stone. I saw Mr. Peabody at Judge
White's, who tells me that there is a prospect of establishing a liberal society at Northampton. Pray,
have you read the correspondence of the people and
Mr. Tucker? I am no partisan of any sect, but I
must rejoice in seeing any progress towards the conviction that Christianity is indeed "*glad tidings of
great joy,*" and that in its original purity it was a
very different thing from the system that is popu-
larly preached, and which is still received as reasonable and scriptural by men and women who in other
respects are sensible and correct in their judgments.
When shall we learn that without the spirit of Christ
we are none of his? . . .

CAMBRIDGE, *May* 4, 1825.

MY DEAR MOTHER, — . . . The prospects of professional success and usefulness appear brighter every
day. There is an unexampled call from all parts of
the country for our students, and a disposition manifested to hear what we consider more useful and
practical, if not more able preaching than can elsewhere be obtained. For my own part, I am more
and more grateful to a kind Providence which directed me to Cambridge, where I have learned those
views of religion at once so attractive and lovely, so
simple, scriptural, and reasonable, — affording such
motives to holiness, such consolation in sorrow, such

hope in death. I trust I am not becoming a partisan nor a bigot. I have suffered enough, and too much, in sustaining those characters, in earlier, more inexperienced, and more ignorant years ; but I have no prospects of earthly happiness more inviting than that of preaching the truth, with the humble hope of being instrumental in impressing it on the mind with greater force, purity, and effect than I could do with any other than my present conviction. I feel bound to my profession, — so much so that you will not be surprised when I inform you that I deemed it right to decline the appointment of mathematical tutor, with an emolument of $700, which was recently offered me. I presume and hope that none of my friends can regret what may appear at first as a pecuniary sacrifice, but what a broad view of the future clearly convinces me was necessary, and ultimately can be of no disadvantage.

CAMBRIDGE, *December* 6, 1825.

DEAR MARIANNE, — I am now very pleasantly situated and delightfully employed, with responsible and difficult labor enough to keep me thoughtful and awake, and intervals of rest to show me that the relaxation purchased by fatigue is by far the best. Father will think my habits are somewhat improving when he hears that I rise two hours before the sun these cold mornings, and never sleep between-while. I am very glad that I accepted the office I am in, as it does not interfere with my professional views, and gives me the consciousness that, instead of being a burden to others I am making myself useful, and instead of being dependent I am earning my bread actually by the sweat of my brow, and it gives me the prospect, at the end of the year, of having laid up in this world's goods a handsome store, for a boy. Still I had rather by far preach, which I hope I shall soon be able to do. We have a fortnight's vacation at Christmas, at which time I intend to " come home," though I do most heartily abhor the process of riding a hundred miles a day in a stage-coach.

CAMBRIDGE, *May* 3, 1826.

My dear Marianne, — . . . I could have wished, for more reasons than one, that mother might find it in her heart to accompany father, as her Boston friends are very desirous to see her, as the journey might benefit her health, and as I myself have various matters of *grave import,* which it would gratify me to hear her discourse upon with her motherly wisdom and sympathy. What these matters are *you* perhaps can conjecture. I shall not unfold them until I am brought, in the gradual progress of events, unto this page of my letter. Well, I have come to this point. In your last letter you asked me what were my prospects on the subject which was nearest to my earthly happiness ; *then*, I should have answered, all was black darkness. Now, my dearest Marianne, by a most unexpected train of events, the obstacles to our affection are removed ; a just regard to prudence does not forbid us to cherish an attachment which has long been the secret idol of our

3

hearts ; and yesterday our circle of dear friends were edified by the intelligence of a new engagement! The details of all this I shall hereafter explain. You will know this being whose influence over me for the year past has so much elevated, strengthened, and refined my character. You will entirely sympathize with me. I cannot now write to my parents, who, I am sure, cannot disapprove the step I have taken, when you expound to them all the circumstances, — which I wish you to do as copiously as you can. The whole matter meets with the most surprising approbation and sympathy from the whole society of Cambridge. The most just, proper, natural, fit, reasonable, delightful connection, say they, that has been known for a long time. My father may, perhaps, think that it would have been more prudent for me to have deferred this consummation until my prospects in an uncertain and trying profession were more definite. To this I have to say, my wisest friends assert that my prospects of professional success, in the highest sense of the term, are tolerably fair, — so much so as entirely to justify this arrangement. What can be depended upon still more, I say myself that for nine years I have relied upon the blessing of a kind Providence given to my own personal, active, patient efforts. In this I have not been disappointed, and it is the course which I fully intend to pursue. It has never been my wish, you all know, to be a rich man, nor what the world calls a great man, but to be a respected, useful, and happy man. And this connection, which is founded not upon any romantic or sudden passion, but upon great respect for intellectual power, moral worth, deep and true Christian piety, and peculiar refinement and dignity of character, promises, I think, to advance me in the best way in this life, and to aid me, above all, in the great end of life, the preparation for heaven. My mother will recollect her great admiration of Dr. Jackson. You will inform her how deeply he is interested, how valuable his friendship, how paternal his advice.

Truly your own brother, GEORGE.

CAMBRIDGE, *August* 25, 1826.

MY DEAR MARIANNE, — I received a letter from you, — a singular rarity, — which I fully believe I answered soon after the occurrence of the auspicious event; but as I have had no returns from Greenfield, a slight suspicion glances over my mind that instead of actually replying to your letter I mistook the will for the deed. Is it so? . . . I begin to preach at Purchase Street on the next Lord's Day; I have then an invitation to renew my engagement at Chauncy Place for an indefinite time; and lastly, a Macedonian cry is heard from Baltimore, " Come over and help us," to which I do not turn the deaf adder's ear, but partially engage to spend some weeks of the winter in that benighted city. I wash my hands of this college on the first day of October next; and hope from that time to eschew the delightful task of directing the young idea in all its various ramifications, and to turn my attention to the nobler labor

of influencing grown men on the most important
subjects. . . .

On his leaving Cambridge, in 1826, he was
at once ordained pastor of a Unitarian society
gathered expressly for him in what was then a
respectable part of Boston. The new meeting-
house at the corner of Purchase and Pearl
Streets, near Griffin's Wharf, where the tea-
ships lay in the old time, was built for its use.
It was a remarkably unattractive structure of
stone, with a small belfry on the top. The inside was as homely as the outside. It was capable of holding about three hundred people.
The corner-stone was laid on the 7th of September, 1825. On that occasion Henry Ware
delivered an address, in which he described the
building to be erected as " not magnificent, but
simple and unostentatious like the faith to which
it is devoted ; " spoke of " the great principles
of the Reformation," "the right of private judgment," and added, "No articles of faith shall
call in question the sufficiency of the Scriptures ; " " Our platform is as wide and generous
as the spirit of our religion itself ; " " If it were
possible in this disturbed day, we could long
and hope that here might be neutral ground.
The day [for this] is coming at length." In
conclusion he said: "Where the heavens now
swell above us, declaring their Maker's glory.

shall soon be interposed a roof of human work-manship, beneath which shall be declared the brighter glory of his redeeming love. We shall intercept the light of yonder sun, whose beams shall no more fall upon this floor; but the more reviving beams of the 'Sun of Righteousness' shall rest there without a cloud. The dews of night shall come down upon this spot no more, and the winds of the ocean shall henceforth be excluded; but the dews of divine grace, as we trust, shall plenteously visit it, and the gentle breathings of the Holy Spirit shall never cease to shed upon it life and peace; and from this place, where now, perhaps, for the first time, the voice of Christian worship has ascended to heaven, there shall forever go up, to the end of time, incense and a pure offering from multi-tudes of humble and believing hearts. Let us go hence with this persuasion."

Ah, how short is the keenest human vision! The multitude never came; the "respectable' people gradually left that quarter of the town, which was rapidly occupied by the dwellers in tenement houses. In less than twenty-five years the building was sold to the Catholics for thirty thousand dollars; the fire of 1872 swept it away, and now nothing remains of the church so hopefully planted. The leather interest has taken possession of the site so poetically dedi

cated to the uses of religion, and the visitor in
that region recalls the words addressed to Shy-
lock in the well known trial scene, " Not on thy
soul, but on thy sole."

The dedication took place August 24, 1826 ;
the ordination followed on the 8th of November. It is evidence of the promise of the new
ministry that the president of Harvard College,
Dr. Kirkland, preached the sermon ; that Dr.
Lowell made the prayer of ordination ; that
Dr. Ware gave the charge. The other clergymen officiating, Alexander Young and Ezra S.
Gannett, were then less known. The young
pastor began his career under brave though
"conservative" auspices.

BOSTON, *November* 26, 1826.

MY DEAR MOTHER, — . . . I am just beginning
to feel at home in my new habitation in Williams
Street, and on many accounts I find it a most desirable situation. The family are everything that I could
wish, and are more devoted to the task of making
me comfortable than one could expect from strangers.
I am in a very central spot, not far from my church,
in the midst of my people, contiguous to all my
haunts, such as the Athenæum, bookstores, etc., and
at the same time it is quiet and retired as the country ; and I can sit and study, near indeed to the busy
world, but undisturbed by its noise, and almost, I
might say, out of the reach of its temptations. My

rooms are pleasant, and furnished in a style of simple neatness, which is as agreeable to my feelings as it is to my circumstances. . .

I have become acquainted with several families in my society, and am better pleased than I at first expected. They are chiefly from the middling classes of society, but I have not yet learned that intelligence and piety are confined to any one class. I am sure of this, that what little experience I have had in the more elevated walks will not here be lost, and 1 trust I may be able to communicate some good influence from the habits of feeling which prevail in a different sphere. I am pretty well satisfied that I shall be happier in the city than I could ever be in the country. I have access to sources of improvement and enjoyment here which I could not have elsewhere, and without which I should feel that something important was wanting. My people are particularly kind to me, and seem disposed to receive all my attempts to move them with real indulgence. I shall try not to be unworthy of their good-will. My health is excellent, and I hope I shall be able to preserve it without much difficulty. I find that preaching agrees with my constitution, and on Monday morning I am as free from fatigue as if I had been idle the day before.   Affectionately your son,

G. RIPLEY.

BOSTON, January 9, 1827.

. . . My hands are full of labor, and my heart with cares for my own people, who, although a little band,

demand a great deal of my time and all of my **atten**
tion. There is a great attention to religion at this
moment throughout the city, and I feel it a bounden
duty to do what I can to promote it, and to direct the
excitement into a proper channel. I administered
the communion for the first time yesterday, and admitted nine to my church, for some of whom I feel a
peculiar interest, as they have been led to the step
under the influence of my preaching. I am gratified
at the serious impressions I find produced, because
they assure me of the adaptation of rational religion
to the needs and sorrows of all conditions of men.
It has been reproached as a faith merely for men of
intellect and taste. It is so, but it also speaks loudly
to the poor and uneducated, as I have had ample
proof.

BOSTON, *February* 14, 1827.

MY DEAR MOTHER, — I have little to say about
myself but that I am quietly peering about the streets
and lanes of the city, dropping the good seeds of Christian truth wherever I find a prepared mind, and once
a week enforcing what I say in private by a more
elaborate argument in public. My society is growing
tranquilly by my side. It is now quite an infant, and
needs gentle nursing, but I hope it will live and advance to the stature of a perfect man.

Yours affectionately, G. R.

Later in this year Mr. Ripley was married to
the lady referred to in the letters, Miss Sophia
Willard Dana, daughter of Francis Dana, of

Cambridge, and from that time lived in what is now Chauncy Street. The union was an exceedingly happy one, a union of mind and heart, spoken of by one who knew them both as " an ideal union." There was entire sympathy in all things.

These were the palmy days of Unitarianism. Societies were formed in different parts of the city; meeting-houses were built; money was raised; missionaries were employed. In that decade the " Ministry at Large" established three chapels: one in Warren Street, one in Pitts Street, and one in Suffolk Street. Dr. Channing, assisted by Mr. Gannett, was preaching in Federal Street; Henry Ware in Hanover Street, F. W. P. Greenwood at King's Chapel. J. G. Palfrey in Brattle Street, Francis Parkman in Hanover Street, Alexander Young in Summer Street, John Pierpont in Hollis Street, Charles Lowell in Lynde Street, Samuel Barrett in Chambers Street, N. L. Frothingham in Chauncy Place, M. I. Motte in Washington Street; James Walker was at Charlestown, Caleb Stetson was at Medford, John Pierce was at Brookline.

Unitarianism had but recently become aware of its existence as a distinct form of the Protestant faith. The habit of free inquiry, once formed, went steadily but silently on, ques-

tioning doctrines, criticising texts, examining
grounds of belief, disputing fundamental dogmas, till, unconsciously, the whole position was
altered. The records of the First Church in
Boston, now more than two hundred and fifty
years old, nowhere intimate that its harmony
was disturbed ; its members chose pastors from
generation to generation without the least difficulty on the score of doctrinal belief, though its
actual minister was one of the foremost teachers
of the so-called " Liberal " school. Mr. Channing's celebrated sermon at the ordination of
Jared Sparks in Baltimore was preached in
1819. The discussion began immediately after,
— Channing taking issue with Dr. Miller of
Princeton, Norton standing up against Moses
Stuart on the question between unity and trin-
ity, Ware facing Dr. Woods as an assailant of
the dogmas of Calvinism.

The Unitarianism of the period we are considering was a dignified form of Christianity, —
sober, thoughtful, serious. It was the religion
of the most intellectual men in the community,
— men like Judge Shaw, Judge Story, Judge
White, — who clung to Christianity with the
tenacious hold of an honest reverence and a
strong conviction. Its historical foundations
they regarded as established ; its founder they
revered as a miraculously authenticated teach

er; they cherished a sentiment of deep rational piety, principles of strict personal morality, and a remarkably high standard of public virtue. They knew nothing of theological subtleties or critical refinements. Here and there a preacher laid vehement stress on points of controversial theology ; now and then a congregation was asked to listen more often than was necessary to prosaic homilies on texts of Scripture, or to discourses on personal morals ; but in the main the style of pulpit administration was devout and spiritual. "Sensational" sermons were not in vogue ; a quiet, even strain of public speech, manly and elevating, prevailed. The " water of life," if cold, was pure ; if not sparkling, it was fresh. There was no fanaticism, little enthusiasm ; but of superstition there was absolutely none. Both ministers and people were persuaded that they could give a reason for the faith that was in them and out of them. Rational they may have been, to a fault. They had lost the sense of mystery ; they put thought before feeling ; substituted sight for insight ; set knowledge in advance of faith. But they were high-minded, full of fear toward God and of love toward the Saviour. They read their Bibles with reverence, said their prayers morning and evening, and kept holy the Lord's Day. The spirit of skepticism was not in them. Of

" philosophy," — whether German, French, or English, — they were as innocent as new-born babes. In their view the clerical profession was exalted above all others ; the minister was a man set apart. They had not fairly begun to express dissatisfaction with the regular dispen- sation of the Word. The modern spirit of in- dividualism, which so often arrays the pew against the pulpit, had not risen to its present stature. Occasional murmurings were heard against this preacher because he did not "draw;" against that one because he was inattentive in the way of parish calls ; against a third because he was too young, or too flowery, or too heed- less of the proprieties, or too unattractive to those who wore the first-class bonnets, the red caps, or the white wigs : but, on the whole, so- cieties were docile. There was no schism and no threat of schism in the body. Theodore Parker's disturbing sermon at South Boston was not preached till 1841 ; and even that was heard without alarm. Mr. Emerson left the ministry in 1832, because he could not admin- ister the rite of communion. So unsuspecting of danger were the leaders of the sect that in 1834 the Association printed as a tract James Walker's admirable address, entitled "The Phi- losophy of Man's Spiritual Nature in regard to the Foundations of Faith," in which doctrines of a "transcendental" complexion were advanced. The "Liberal" movement had not entered on its third stage when George Ripley was ordained.

He was no unbeliever, no skeptic, no innovator in matters of opinion or observance, but a quiet student, a scholar, a man of books, a calm, bright-minded, high-souled thinker; believing, hopeful, social, sunny, but absorbed in philosophical pursuits. Well does the writer of these lines recall the vision of a slender figure, wearing in summer the flowing silk robe, in winter the long dark blue cloak, of the profession, walking with measured step from his residence in Rowe Place towards the meeting-house in Purchase Street. The face was shaven clean; the brown hair curled in close, crisp ringlets; the face was pale as if with thought; gold-rimmed spectacles concealed the black eyes; the head was alternately bent and raised. No one could have guessed that the man had in him the fund of humor in which his friends delighted, or the heroism in social reform which, a few years later, amazed the community. He seemed a sober, devoted minister of the gospel, formal, punctilious, ascetic, a trifle forbidding to the stranger. But even then the new thoughts of the age were at work within him.

On the fly-leaf of his commonplace book Milton, Cicero, and Bacon are quoted in praise of philosophy, — Bacon's language being given with emphasis: " Life without pursuit is a vague and languid thing." " Cicero gives it as a high commendation to Cato *that he embraced philosophy*, not for the purpose of disputing, as most do, *but of living philosophically.*" He had a remarkably fine library, containing many French and German books: much of Kant, Schleiermacher, Herder, De Wette, Cousin, Jouffroy; something of Hegel; Schopenhauer's "Die Welt als Wille und Vorstellung" (1819); the latest known volumes of biblical criticism; Paulus, Bauer, Tholuck, Lücke; Bertholdt's " Einleitung," Winer's " Handbuch der Theologischen Literatur," Bretschneider, Ammon, Reinhard, Ritter; histories of philosophy, both general and special; Constant, Vico, Fichte, Cabanis, Eichhorn; a few books, now forgotten, about the origin of Christianity; a little of Goethe and Schiller, Luther's Werke, Baumgarten-Crusius; Heydenreich's " Betrachtungen," and " Natur und Gott, nach Spinoza," Wieland's " Ueber Wunder,' Gfrörer's " Giordano Bruno," and miscellaneous works in morals and philosophy. Some of his books were imported, but many of them were brought from abroad by a young American, who studied divinity at Cambridge, became an enthusiastic disciple of Dr.

Spurzheim, went to Germany to study anatomy, lost his Christian faith, returned to America, bringing a library with him, and, while still comparatively young, died in Boston. Mr. Ripley studied his books faithfully, and made his reading enrich his mind. None of the critical or metaphysical lore got into his sermons, which were simple, clear, calm, systematic, not eloquent, but pervaded by a keen, lambent light, and in passages animated by a singular intellectual glow, as of an aurora borealis. Two or three remain to us in manuscript. They breathe and convey the air of the new ideas, but are wholly destitute of controversial heat, and betray no sign of the existence of a different philosophy from his own. One of them, preached in 1837, entitled " Common Sense in the Affairs of Religion " (marked 419), assumes the presence of a universal sentiment which guides men through the devious ways of faith, and delivers, or should deliver, them from the dangers that lurk in the path ; securing to them unanimity in opinion, liberty of conscience, a spirit of aspiration and progress, and a prevailing interest in spiritual things. The discourse ends with a noble strain of appeal in behalf of freedom in thought and life. Another sermon, on " Jesus Christ, the same Yesterday, To-day, and Forever," contends that the history of man is a religious history; that religious truths always have existed; that "the religious ideas which were set forth by Jesus Christ, as they had been displayed before in other forms, still exert an efficient influence on the soul of man;" that, in their essential form, they will never cease to influence human souls. This was a favorite sermon. First preached in 1834, it was repeated in 1839, delivered nine or ten times to other congregations, given twice on Christmas occasions, once at an installation, once at O. A. Brownson's. It contains the substance of Theodore Parker's sermon on the "Transient and Permanent in Christianity," but stated so luminously, persuasively, and in such uncritical terms as to awaken no dissent. It was the word of a hearty believer, unconcerned with the thankless task of denying, which was laid on the reformer of Spring Street.

George Ripley was a disciple of the intuitive philosophy then coming into authority among liberal scholars in Europe and America. The philosophy called "transcendental," which claimed 'or human nature a spiritual faculty, by virtue cf which truths of the spiritual order could be clearly discerned, was coming into favor. The assumption was precisely the opposite to that set up by theologians who maintained that spiritual knowledge came from above by special grace, and was bestowed on believers as a sign of their redemption from the thraldom of the natural mind. That debased humanity; this exalted it. That regarded man as depraved; this regarded him as puissant. That classed human beings with the creatures of sin; this ranked them with the angels. Transcendentalism, in its full form, was a deification of Nature But with its earliest teachers and prophets — Channing, Emerson, Walker, Ripley, Parker — it signified merely a new, broad, ideal faith, unsectarian, spiritual, earnest. George Ripley believed, without misgiving, in religion as a gift from heaven, and in Christianity as a divine communication to man. In the discourse to which reference has just been made, he says: "We can have no doubt that religion will always be perpetuated by the same causes which first gave it existence. We regard it as an emanation from the Eternal Mind." "These attributes [eternity, unchangeableness] are applied to our Saviour, because his mind was so filled and penetrated with the power of religious truth as to be identical with it as existing in the Divine Mind, — as to be the Truth, as well as the way and the life." He constantly calls Christ "Saviour," speaking of him with deepest reverence as the highest of all the soul's prophets. His views on the subject of inspiration,

4

then beginning to agitate the thinking world, are expressed with clearness and candor in the remarkable review of Martineau's "Rationale of Religious Inquiry," published in the "Christian Examiner" for November, 1836, — the same year, it may be observed, in which appeared the first volume of Norton's "Genuineness of the Gospels," and Furness's "Remarks on the Four Gospels." His position is that "necessary and universal truths" are divinely implanted in man's spiritual constitution, like the axioms of geometry, intuitively recognized as true. Touching Christ, he writes: "His soul was a sea of light. All that was human in the Son of the Virgin; all that belonged to his personality as a Jewish teacher; all that marks the secondary, derived, and fallible in the nature of man, as distinguished from the primitive, the infallible, and divine, was swallowed up, and, as it were, annihilated in the fullness of the Spirit which dwelt in him, in those kingly ideas of Truth and Good which sustain the authority of the Eternal Throne, and authenticated the man of Nazareth as the Son of God, the visible tabernacle of the Word which was made flesh and dwelt among us."

These would be accepted now as moderate opinions, though when spoken they were pronounced dangerous. How far they were altered or dropped in after life it would not be quite safe to say. The philosophical basis on which they rested remained unmoved to the end, as his papers in the "Tribune," especially his review of Bascom's "Comparative Psychology," will bear witness. In the summer of 1878 he read with great interest Hartmann's "Philosophy of the Unconscious," making notes as he read. These notes contain evidence, less in the form of actual expression than in the selection of passages quoted, of his adherence to the intuitive system of thought. He was in no sense or degree a materialist, and, though connecting himself with an independent society of a decidedly radical school, he held fast his faith in beliefs which his minister dismissed. His appeal was still to consciousness and the soul. Of doctrines he had little to say, being content to see them change and pass away, but the substance of spiritual conviction he retained to the last.

Mr. Ripley called himself a child of Channing, and so he was in the sense of sharing his essential views. Channing, too, was accused of 'rash speculation," perhaps because he would utter words like the following : "We believe that the human mind is akin to that intellectual energy which gave birth to nature, and consequently that it contains within itself the seminal and prolific principles from which nat-

ure sprung." [1] A child of that great spiritual
prophet — that sayer of thoughts which expressed the spirit of his age, and stirred the
souls of men on either side of the Atlantic Ocean
— he certainly was not. He was lacking in the
gift of thrilling speech. His convictions did not
fall glowing from his lips. His ideas, though
clear, cogent, and earnestly put forth, did no
execution. In a small room, among personal
friends, on his own themes, and following his
own impulse, he was eloquent, persuasive, en-
chanting ; but in a meeting-house, on a formal
occasion, before a mixed audience, on impersonal subjects, he was unimpassioned, almost
cold. He must have his hearer within arm's
length ; then his full power was felt. Individually his parishioners were much attached
to him. They found him delightful in their
homes ; a true friend, sympathetic and consoling, more than ready in all cases of need with
counsel and assistance. For many years after
his ministry ceased, those who had known him
as a pastor spoke of him with a depth of affection which nothing but faithful service could
justify or explain. A few still live to speak
tender words in his memory.

There is an impression abroad that Mr. Ripley was an uninteresting preacher, but such was

[1] *Sermons*, 1830, 8vo, p. 189.

not the universal opinion. During a visit to Ohio in 1838, his discourses, especially those which he delivered without notes, excited great enthusiasm. Men of mark flocked about him, urged him to prolong his stay with them, spoke of his sermons as the finest they had ever listened to. One man, the agent of a canal company, sent travelling passes to him and his wife. Another expressed his willingness to subscribe handsomely for the maintenance of such an administration of religion. Like many men, he felt the influence of new people and places, and spoke most winningly when " off duty."

He was often called on to perform services for friends in the ministry. At the ordination of J. S. Dwight, at Northampton (May 20 1840), he preached on the " Claims of the Age on the Work of the Evangelist," saying, in the course of the sermon (it was on the eve of the Brook Farm experiment), " The true work of the evangelist at the present day is to bring the religion of society into accordance with the religion of Christ." In 1837 he presented the fellowship of the churches to his young friend Theodore Parker. On the 4th of July, 1839, he offered prayer at the public celebration in the Odeon. He was constant in his attendance at the ministers' meetings, and on all occasions of discussion or of conversation, in which matters of social, philosophical, or religious concern were brought up. At such times he was always listened to with interest, and easily held his own among eloquent, wise, instructed men. None were brighter, wittier, heartier, or more suggestive than he, always frank, always sparkling. He was a member of the first transcendental coterie that met in Cambridge, the nucleus of all future organizations.

The first meeting of the Transcendental Club was at his house, on the 19th of September, 1836. There were present, beside the host, R. W. Emerson, F. H. Hedge, C. Francis, J. F. Clarke, and A. B. Alcott. It was a preliminary meeting, to see how far it might be possible for earnest minds to meet and communicate their thoughts without formality. At the second meeting, O. A. Brownson and C. A. Bartol were present. At that time theology was a theme of general interest and discussion. Dr. Beecher, Andrews Norton, Dr. Channing, were names on all lips. Mr. Emerson, in December, gave the first of a series of lectures in Boston, the subjects being " History," " Art," " Science," " Literature," " Politics," " Religion," "Society," " Trades and Professions," " Manners," " Ethics," " The Present Age " (two lectures). In 1837, Caleb Stetson, Theodore Parker, Margaret Fuller (who came to Boston to reside in 1836), and Elizabeth Peabody, were added to the club; later, Thomas T. Stone joined it. It is worth noting that the Massachusetts Board of Education was established almost contemporaneously with the club. At the meetings, Mr. Emerson was usually present; Mr. Hedge, too, before he went to Bangor. The topics debated turned on a few central ideas: Law, Truth, Individuality, the Personality of God. The last point came up in connection with matters pertaining to Theology, Revelation, Inspiration, Providence. An extreme reaction from Puritan conceptions set in, leading some to the verge of pantheism, and to a belief in the sufficiency of the human mind to itself, in all emergencies. The conversation was at all times earnest and elevated, though there was warm discussion over some of the views submitted.

Theodore Parker describes Mr. Ripley at this time as discussing, along with Dr. Channing, " with great power of thought and richness of eloquence," the question of the progress of civilization. " Had the conversation of this evening," he records, " been written out by Plato, it would equal any of his beautiful dialogues." The conversation referred to was held in the rooms of Mr. Jonathan Phillips, at the Tremont House. At a subsequent meeting Mr. Ripley is instanced as taking exception to the impersonal conception of God put forth by Mr. Emerson in a remarkable lecture. This was in February, 1838. Theodore Parker was introduced to Mr. Ripley by his classmate, George E. Ellis. An intimacy grew up which continued close till Parker's death, though their ministerial connection was short. The two were drawn together by a deeply rooted sympathy in philosophical ideas, by a common philanthropical aim, and by an irrepressible buoyancy of spirit. They walked and talked by the day. In 1838, in the early time of Parker's ministry, Ripley and his wife spent a week with him at West Roxbury. The visit was remembered fondly many years afterward. "We were full of joy and laughter all the time of their visit." When lying ill in Boston, after a surgical operation, Parker wrote, November 1, 1858: "Many thanks for your friendship, *which never fails.* If we could lie under the great oak-tree at West Roxbury, or ride about its wild little lanes together, I should soon be entirely well, for the vigor of your mind would inspire strength even into my body. But I must do without that, only too thankful to have had it once." Almost a year later, January 10, 1859, the mortally sick man wrote in pencil from his bed in Exeter Place: "Many thanks, my dear George, to *you.* I never told you the service you rendered me in 1836 — and so on. Your words of advice, of profound philosophic thought, and still more, of lofty cheer, did me great good. I count your friendship as one of the brightest spots in my life, which has had a deal of handsome sunshine. God bless you."

They were very different men. One was engrossed in books; the other was full of action. One was contemplative, quiet, thoughtful; the other was impetuous. One was silent; the other was outspoken. One was cautious to the verge of timidity; the other was bold to the verge of rashness. One was a thinker, taking no part in agitation, political or social; the other was a reformer, eager to apply his ideas to laws and institutions. But their faith in one another was constant. The following letters show how Parker's love was reciprocated.

TRIBUNE OFFICE, N. Y., *February* 28, 1856.

MY DEAR THEODORE, — The new edition of your brave book came to hand yesterday, and need I say your friendly and tender words did not fail to touch my heart. Certain it is that from my first acquaintance with you, my sympathy was won by your robust devotion to truth, and your cordial, overflowing geniality; but that you could have ever received any encouragement in your lofty career from one so distant from your orbit, would be incredible to those

who did not know that you combine a woman's soft-
ness of feeling with your manly "heart of oak." But
let that be as it may, our friendship has weathered
many a winter and summer, and only grown brighter
from the test of time; and it is always a pleasant
thought to me when I reflect on how little I have
brought to pass for my day and generation, that at
least I have been loyal to the principles of truth and
freedom, which have ripened in you to such a bounti-
ful harvest of accomplishment. I can sincerely say
that I rejoice in your success as if it had been my
own; and perhaps you will not deem it strange if I
tell you how perpetually grateful I am to you for
presenting to the world an example of a true man, in
the midst of the dwarfs, mountebanks, satyrs, and
monkeys, which make modern society so mean and
false and hollow and repulsive.

I have scarcely looked into your volume, and
probably should not find my ancient interest in its
contents. I cannot digest any religion but the worship of the Eternal Word, as expounded in many
" colloquies divine " with you; but how little man is
prepared for such a pure faith, I am too deeply sensible. Still, if the world is not an audacious " quiz of
nature," as Emerson holds, I think all creeds must
ultimately be merged in this " positive," or, as you
would say, " absolute " religion.

I depend on seeing you next week, and presume
our hospitable and reverential Brace has a breakfast
in contemplation.

Good-by, and believe me ever faithfully yours,

GEORGE RIPLEY.

MY DEAR THEODORE, — I truly rejoice that you are able to report so good an account of yourself. Heaven send that your complete cure may be as speedy and effectual as your best friends could wish. How I regret that I have no nice country house, in which I could tempt you to spend the languid hours of convalescence, and return (not repay) your kindness to me on a similar occasion, just twenty years ago next summer. It was only the other day my wife was speaking of our enjoyment of that little episode, which was, in fact, the causal and immediate antecedent of Brook Farm, with all its wondrous experiences.

I have looked pretty carefully into the "Intuitive Morals." It is a remarkable production for any one, especially for a woman, and a British woman. She sees clearly the absolute character of the primary idea of right, and argues the question manfully. Her logic is as genuine as her learning, which is almost unique. The second volume is a falling off; but it is only the change from pure theory to application, in which minds of her cast seldom do their best. You are happy to know such a person. She cannot be frowzy and snuffy, like some lady theologians on our side of the water.

Don't let your amanuensis forget me, but keep me supplied with bulletins ; and with kind remembrance to your household saints, believe me yours ever,

GEORGE RIPLEY.

New York, *January* 15, 1859.

My dear Theodore, — You were very kind to write to me from your sick-bed, which I trust will soon be changed into the couch of convalescence. With your great fund of vitality I cannot but anticipate a speedy restoration to your usual labors ; but I am sure you cannot be anxious on this point, as you have already done such a day's work in the harvest of humanity, and even in the midst of life have gathered such a store of autumn sheaves.

Whether you go to the West Indies or to Europe, or to some Ultima Thule yet more unknown, you will be followed by the benedictions and grateful sympathies of many loving hearts, who have received from you their first impulses to truly divine and beautiful things.

My wife bids me give you her kindest remembrances, and the assurance of ancient friendship, while I remain, dear Theodore, ever your faithful friend,   George Ripley.

Before Parker's controversial period began his friend had left the ministry. At the time of their first acquaintance the future heresiarch was unsuspected. He was writing diligently in " The Examiner " about Cudworth, Sir Thomas More, St. Bernard, Olshausen, Gesenius, Du Cange, Matter's " Gnosticism," and other saintly or scholastic matters. A literary notice of works, then recently published in Germany (May, 1839), reports a third edition o:

Strauss's " Leben Jesu," also an essay by Strauss
on the " Transient and Permanent in Christianity," printed in a periodical called the " Frei-
hafen." Parker's article on Strauss in " The
Examiner" for July, 1840, is unnecessarily
conservative. Strauss's method is turned to
ridicule by being applied to the history of
American Independence. " The Examiner " for
January, 1839, contains a paper by Parker on
Ackerman's " Christliche in Plato," the tone of
which is not merely conservative but highly
eulogistic of the peculiar excellences of the
Christian religion.

During this period Ripley was doing his best
to make his own ministry effective, by promot-
ing interest among the members of his society
in each other, in the Unitarian cause, in general charity. But all efforts were vain ; nothing succeeded. The situation of the meeting-
house was unfortunate ; the neighborhood deteriorated ; money fell short ; the minister had
misgivings in regard to his fitness for professional work. The correspondence printed below
explains the situation, and prepares for the next
step in a new career.

NORTHAMPTON, *May* 21, 1840.

MY RESPECTED FRIENDS, — I learn with regret
that the pecuniary affairs of the church are not in a
prosperous condition. I also understand that the

means of providing funds to meet the expenses is now the subject of discussion.

Under these circumstances I feel that it is due both to you and myself, to express my own views with the perfect frankness which has always marked our intercourse.

Our connection was formed in the beginning with a full view of the difficulties which it involved; the most sanguine friends of the church were not confident of success; and on the whole I do not know that our prosperity has been less than we had reason to anticipate. There have always, however, been many discouragements; and at times these have been so great, that nothing but a sense of the kindness I have received at your hands, and the conviction that my best endeavors were due to you so long as they were desired, has prevented me from requesting to be discharged from your service.

I cannot then avoid deeming this the proper occasion to say that if the support of my office should be thought burdensome or inexpedient in the deliberate judgment of your body and the society which you represent, it would be my desire to relinquish it. If your interests can be better promoted by other hands, I wish that they may assume that trust. I have now labored with you for nearly fourteen years; I have done what I could to accomplish the purposes of our connection; and under the present relation it is not likely that my ministry can be essentially different from what it has been; I do not feel that I can do more in the time to come than I have done in the time past.

With these convictions, I am bound to give you the option of preserving the present connection. It must be a matter of free will and of good will on both sides, or it can be productive of no pleasant fruits. I beg, therefore, that you will discuss the subject as far as you shall deem it necessary, with the same freedom as if the question were now to be taken on my settlement for the first time.

In making this communication, I trust too much to your candor to suppose that it will be ascribed to a weariness with my duties or a want of attachment to my society. I wish to consult the common good, without peculiar reference to myself. On former occasions I have felt bound to you by ties which I could not prevail on myself to break. This same feeling remains on my part; but I shall cheerfully adopt a different course if I were persuaded that it would meet your wishes or be for your advantage; and in whatever sphere I might be placed, I should not cease to rejoice in your welfare and to be grateful for your friendship.

With sincere regard, I am, my respected friends,
> Your faithful and affectionate servant,
> > GEO. RIPLEY.

MY DEAR FRIENDS, — You were informed on the last Lord's Day that I should take this opportunity to present to you a communication in regard to the correspondence which was held in the month of May last, between the proprietors of the church and myself. I had thought that this course was due to you on account of your personal interest in the subject, and of the intrinsic fitness that you should be fully informed of everything that belongs to the pastoral relation, which you help to sustain. It is those who attend upon his preaching with whom the minister has the most intimate concern ; he knows no distinction in the body of worshippers between proprietors and others ; but the moment a family or an individual becomes a part of his congregation, a spiritual relation is established between him and their souls. I accordingly address this communication to you, with the assurance that you will listen to it with the same candor with which you have always received the frankest disclosures of my mind from this place.

In my letter to the proprietors of the church, in May, I made use of the following language : "If the support of my office should be thought burdensome or inexpedient in the deliberate judgment of your body and the society which you represent, it would be my desire to relinquish it. If your interests can be better promoted by other hands, I wish that they may assume the trust. I have now labored with you for nearly fourteen years ; I have done what I could to accomplish the purpose of our connection, and, under the present relation, it is not likely that my ministry can be essentially different from what it has been. I do not feel that I can do more in the time to come than I have in the time past. With this conviction, I am bound to give you the option of preserving our present connection. It must be a matter

of free-will and of good-will on both sides, or it can
be productive of no pleasant fruits. I beg, therefore,
that you will discuss the subject, so far as you shall
deem it necessary, with the same freedom as if the
question were now to be taken on my settlement for
the first time." I was induced to make this state
ment, my friends, from a conviction that your prosperity as a society could not be greatly increased by
my labors, under the arrangements which now exist
in most of our churches. I had met you for many
years from Sunday to Sunday ; the thoughts and
feelings, which were perhaps new to many of you
when first presented, had lost much of their freshness ; my own mind had ceased to take a deep interest in many points which we had fully considered
with each other ; while at the same time I was aware
there were others in which I had a deep concern,
which had failed to attract your attention. I was
called upon, notwithstanding, to address nearly the
same individuals, to pursue the same track on which
we had long traveled together, to use great diligence
lest I should depart from the usual sphere of the pulpit, and touch on subjects which, by the general consent of our churches, are banished from the ordinary
meeting of our public assemblies on the Lord's Day.
Such a course must always be productive of depression and embarrassment. Unless a minister is expected to speak out on all subjects which are upper-
most in his mind, with no fear of incurring the charge
of heresy or compromising the interests of his congregation, he can never do justice to himself, to his
5

people, or the truth which he is bound to declare. If it is virtually understood that he is to confine himself to a certain round of familiar topics, that he is to abstain from what are called exciting subjects, from all points on which his hearers may be presumed greatly to differ, he can never speak with the earnestness and life which become the messenger who bears the Word of God on his lips. I was fully sensible that I was suffering from this influence; that I had not strength to resist the formality and coldness which are breathed from the atmosphere of our churches; and that, unless we could all break away from such influences, it was wholly in vain for me to speak any longer in this pulpit. It was my wish, therefore, to leave you perfectly free to make such arrangements as would conduce to your highest welfare. I thought that a change in the administration of religion here would be for our mutual advantage. I did not feel at liberty to propose any important alterations in the principles on which our worship was conducted, while at the same time I was certain that without some change my ministry among you could not be carried on with any vital power.

I will confess, also, that I was somewhat influenced in the conclusion at which I had arrived by the present aspect of the times. This is very different from what it was when I became your minister. In 1826 the Unitarian controversy was in the ascendant. It excited general interest; questions of dogmatic theology were in every one's mouth; and a popular exposition of the arguments from reason and Scripture

.n favor of liberal views always commanded general attention. At the same time, inquiries relating to personal religion were not infrequent; many were aroused from the slumber of worldliness and sin; for the first time, religion became a subject of vast and solemn import to their souls; and the plainest and most elementary instruction on the duties of the Christian life were everywhere welcome. That was a good state of things. It promised well for the future. It awakened the brightest hopes in regard to the practical influence of religion in the community; to the spread of the pure, disinterested, and lovely spirit of charity in the various relations of society; to the visible exhibition of freedom and holiness in the lives of those who had been born from above, and who seemed to share largely in the divine power of the truths which they had embraced. But this state of things it seems could not last forever. It passed away, and a new order of ideas was brought forward. The essential principles of liberal Christianity, as I had always understood them, made religion to consist, not in any speculative doctrine, but in a divine life. They asserted the unlimited freedom of the human mind, and not only the right, but the duty of private judgment. They established the kingdom of God, not in the dead past, but in the living present; gave the spirit a supremacy over the letter; insisted on the necessity of pointing out the corruptions of the church, of sweeping away the traditions which obscured the simplicity of truth, and urged every soul to press on to the highest at

tainment; to forget what was behind, and never to
be kept back from expressing its convictions by the
voice of authority or the fear of man. A portion
of the liberal clergy felt it their duty to carry out
these views; to be faithful to their principles; not to
shrink from their application, but to exercise the freedom which God gave them in the investigation of
truth and the enforcement of its practical results.
They could not linger around the grave of the past.
The experiences of manhood enlarged the conception
of their pupilage. They had been taught that no
system of divinity monopolized the truth, and they
were no more willing to be bound by the prevailing
creed of Boston or Cambridge, than their fathers had
been by the prescription of Rome or Geneva. But
in these conclusions they were divided from some of
their brethren. It was thought dangerous to continue the progress which had been commenced. Liberal churches began to fear liberality, and the most
heretical sect in Christendom to bring the charge of
being so against those who carried out its own principles. They who defended the progress as well as
the freedom of thought were openly denounced as
infidels; various unintelligible names were applied
to them; and, instead of judging the tree by its
fruits, and acknowledging the name of Christian to
all who possessed Christ's spirit and claimed to have
received his revelation, men appealed to the prejudices
of the multitude, and sought to destroy the religious
influence of their brethren, on account of the specu-
'ative opinions which they sincerely believed to be

true and Christian. Now it was with this latter class
that I always found myself. I had a native aversion
to human authority for the soul; truth seemed to me
to be supernatural, and our own perception limited.
I could not stand still; I had faith in man and in
God, and never felt the slightest alarm lest the light
from above should lead into paths of danger. But I
soon found that this spirit could not pass without rebuke. The plainest expositions of Christian truth,
as it seemed to me, were accused of heresy. Every
idea which did not coincide with prevailing opinions,
and many which had heretofore always been received
by liberal chnrches, were considered hostile to church
and state, were spoken of under various appellations
which no man understood, and this caused the unin-
itiated to fear and the good to grieve.

Under these circumstances, my friends, I was unwilling that you should be forced to share in the
odium which might attach to the heresies of your
minister. I knew that subjects of philosophical inquiry could scarce be made interesting or even intel-
ligible to a popular audience; that the pulpit was no
place for them; and hence, though I have always
stated with as much distinctness as I could the results of my investigation that related to religion, you
will bear me witness that I have not often brought
abstract questions before you; that I have spared you
the class of subjects that belong to the student rather
than to the practical church, and which have no bearing on the imprint of the character, or the regeneration of the soul. For this reason, I felt that you

were entitled to the perfect freedom of judging
whether any reputed heresies had impaired the influence of my preaching ; and that, if you suffered from
the effect of any change, of which I was unconscious
myself, you might have an opportunity to declare it.
I knew that my own opinion was the same as when
I entered the ministry ; the views which I cherished
of the Scriptures, of Jesus Christ, of the nature of
man, of the character of religion, of the condition of
society, were identical with those which I have ever
maintained since I began to think for myself; but
the experience of several years has no doubt enlarged
and confirmed them, given them a deeper hold on my
mind, led me to perceive their importance more intensely, shown me the practical conclusions which a
sound logic draws from them, has made me more and
more desirous to communicate them to others, and
to insist on their application to social reform and the
advancement of the age. If these facts had influenced the general tone of my preaching, made me a
different man from what I was when you first knew
me, or in any respects estranged me from your sympathies, I knew that our further connection would be
of no utility, and that justice and candor alike demanded an opportunity for explanation. I wanted
you to understand me precisely as I am, to know the
interest I felt in the movements of the day, which are
met by some with frowns and by others with ridicule,
and by all perhaps with something of that undefined
fear, which any new expression of thought is apt to
excite in minds that have no sense of the conflicts by
which truth is ever won.

There is still another circumstance which had no small weight in leading me to the decision which I announced. I felt that though in many respects I could rejoice in the fruit of my labors, though you bore every external mark of being a prosperous and flourishing society, though my words had not fallen actually on the ground, but had found access to the hearts of some among you, yet I had failed in producing the effects, which, it appears to me, are the best results of the ministry, and without which, ro minister can feel that he fills a noble or a manly sphere. I have always endeavored to awaken and cherish a spirit of mental independence, a love of religious progress, a desire for every man and woman to see the truth with their own eyes and not another's, and to regard the worship of God in spirit and in truth as of more importance than any external compliance. I have had no wish but to see the growth of pure, upright, just, generous, and aspiring souls, as the fruit of my labors. Hence you will know that I have never attempted to play the priest in your church or your houses. I have had no faith in the mock solemnity which is sometimes assumed for effect. I have been as unwilling to exercise the authority which is supposed to belong to the clerical profession, as to permit its exercise on myself; my whole oul shrinks from it either way. I would neither be a despot nor a slave; but I have lived with you as a man with men, as a friend, a brother, an equal, disclaiming any means of influence but those which grow out of sincerity of purpose and the faithful exposition of truth. It has been my desire, from the first moment of our connection until this time, to lead you to think for yourselves. I have endeavored to set an example of this in my own character. I have always maintained that whatever else a minister might do for his people he could not make his own thought, or prayer, or good life, a substitute for theirs; they must take the task into their own hands, and work out their own salvation with fear and trembling. Hence, I have been content with the distinct exhibition of truth; popular excitement has never been my aim. I have felt that I have done all I could do when I had presented a subject in its various bearings to the intelligence and higher sentiments of my hearers. This course, I am aware, has not met with the approbation of all. A more authoritative and zealous mode of preaching has been desired by some individuals; they would have the days of the old priesthood restored, when the clergyman trusted more to his office than to his words, and advanced his opinions as oracles to be submitted to rather than as suggestions to be weighed and considered. I am not sure but that they are right in their views. It may be the case that the pulpit does depend for its efficacy on its elevation above the common herd; that men cannot be addressed from it as equals or friends; that something more than simplicity, earnestness, and good sense, are required to act upon our congregation; and that it is in vain to trust to natural feeling without artificial excitement. But if this be the fact, I can only say that I deeply regret

.t. If it be an objection that a man speaks in the pulpit, as men speak anywhere else, on subjects that deeply interest them, the true man will soon find that he can speak more to the purpose in some other place. It has moreover always been one of my firm est convictions, that we meet in the church on the broadest ground of spiritual equality. The true followers of Jesus are a band of brothers; they compose one family; they attach no importance whatever to the petty distinctions of birth, rank, wealth, and station; but feeling that they are one in the pursuit of truth, in the love of holiness, and in the hope of immortal life, they regard the common differences of the world, by which men are separated from each other, as lighter than the dust of the balance. They look on each other with mutual respect and honor; they have no struggle for preëminence; they have no desire for the chief seats in the synagogue, nor greetings in the markets and the streets; and the poor widow, who leaves the daily toil by which a suffering family is kept from want, to gather with the faithful in the house of worship, is welcomed with as warm a sympathy, and regarded with as sincere affection, and treated with just as much respect, as they who are arrayed in costly robes, and who come from the heights of office or the abodes of luxury, to look up to the common Father, in whose sight a pure heart and clean hands are alone of value. These ideas I have perhaps insisted on more strongly than any others, for they have been near my heart; they are a part of my life; they seem to me to be the very essence of the religion which I was taught The great fact of human equality before God is not one to let the heart remain cold ; it is not a mere speculative abstraction ; it is something more than a watchword for a political party to gain power with, and then do nothing to carry it into practical operation ; it is a deep, solemn, vital truth, written by the Almighty in the laws of our being, announced with terrible distinctness to the oppressor by his beloved Son, and pleaded for by all that is just and noble in the promptings of our nature. Blame me for it if you will, but I cannot behold the degradation, the ignorance, the poverty, the vice, the ruin of the soul, which is everywhere displayed in the very bosom of Christian society in our own city, while men look idly on, without a shudder. I cannot witness the glaring inequalities of condition, the hollow pretension of pride, the scornful apathy with which many urge the prostration of man, the burning zeal with which they run the race of selfish competition, with no thought for the elevation of their brethren, without the sad conviction that the spirit of Christ has well-nigh disappeared from our churches, and that the fearful doom awaits us, " Inasmuch as ye have not done it unto one of the least of these, ye have not done it unto me."

But with these feelings, I fear, I have had little sympathy. They have not been understood. They have been regarded as bearing on political struggles, or having reference to party strife ; and this earnes* defense in public and in private has been construed

into a zeal for questions with which I have had no
concern, and connected me with movements from
which I have always stood aloof. The defense of
humanity is sometimes considered an attack on society; a sense of the evil of prevalent systems a reflection on the character of the men who sustain them;
and the ardent desire to see every one aid in the dignity of an immortal soul, sharing all the benefits
which circumstances permit, be possessed of the
means of the highest spiritual culture, and not destitute of any of the many comforts of life, is con-
founded with the measure of the politician or the in-
trigue of the demagogue. In common with many
others, I know that I have been misunderstood in
this matter. I make no account of this fact in reference to myself; but when a minister of the gospel
cannot show by his life and conduct, by his word and
his works, that he is hostile to all oppression of man
by man, that he values moral worth more than outward condition, that he regards the indulgence of
pride as a sin against the Holy Ghost, and that all
his sympathies are with the down-trodden and suffering poor, without impairing the influence of his labors, I feel that it is time to look at the foundation
on which we stand, and see if it does not suffer from
some defect which threatens its destruction.

With such convictions, my friends, I addressed to
the proprietors of the church the letter which has
led to the present communication. I was persuaded
that we must sooner or later come to a fair understanding with each other. I was aware that there

were certain views on which we did not probably co
incide; and believing that no church, under our present arrangements, admitted that perfect liberty of
thought and expression which I must ever prize as a
part of the human birthright, and which is essential
to all noble and effective utterance, if I had felt myself at liberty so to do, I should have asked at once
to be discharged from your service. But this liberty
I did not feel. I have considered myself bound by
no common ties to this society. I came here in the
inexperience of early youth, called from the retirement and ignorance of a literary life, to form a new
congregation, with no external aid in my favor, but
with many discouraging circumstances to contend
with, and often made to perceive that the responsibilities of the station were greater than I could easily
sustain. Nothing could have sustained me but a firm
reliance on God, and the undeviating kindness and
friendship which I have enjoyed, with scarce an exception, from every individual who has shared in my
ministry. As minister and society we have grown
up together; we have neither of us known any other
pastoral relation, and have stood by each other. I
have surely spared no pains to do you whatever good
was in my power; and I rejoice to testify here in this
place that you have ever been faithful and true to
me; and that I would not accept the ministry over
any congregation I am acquainted with, in exchange
for that which I now bear. The friendships which I
have formed with many of you are such as few enjoy; the intimate acquaintance which I have shared

with all who permitted me this privilege has been a source of the richest satisfaction. I have never entered your doors without being welcomed with expressions of regard. Your familiar intercourse with my household, in days of gladness and of grief, I have deemed one of my brightest honors ; while the remembrance of those with whom I have gone down to the dark valley, whose children, parents, and the companions of their life I now speak to, seem to entwine a new cord around my heart, and to stay my lingering steps, as their benignant faces still hover in our season of worship, and the green sods have not yet faded upon their graves.

It seemed to me, accordingly, that I was bound to take the course which I had decided on ; to leave you the freedom of releasing me if you chose to do so ; that I could not retire from the post where you had placed me, until I saw clearly that such a step would be without injury to you or dishonor to myself.

The letter which was addressed to me by the proprietors, by whom you are represented, was of a character to call for my distinct and grateful acknowledgments. To say that I received it without a sense of the kindness and esteem by which it was dictated, would indicate an insensibility which I do not claim to possess. In that letter the following language is employed, in reply to the communication which I had made : " We hope that you will consent to continue as our pastor, and that we may receive from your official character those lessons of instruction which we value, and in our social relations those marks of kind regard and consolation in private affliction which you are so eminently adapted to give, and which always have been so given as to require our utmost thanks. We beg leave to assure you that we think the continuance of the society in Purchase Street mainly depends on your continuance as pastor, and that, should you leave, a considerable portion of those who have longest been with you, and who have a strong attachment to your character, would also leave; and should these events take place, we do not now perceive how the remainder of the society could, without any considerable accession of numbers, grant that support to a pastor which duty and justice would seem to require of them. In closing this communication, we are sure that we should do our constituents great injustice, did we not assure you of their great personal regard, and that our own regard is no less ardent. We therefore hope and trust that you may be listened to in future with the same pleasure and interest with which you were heard in the commencement of your ministry."

The views thus expressed, my friends, were confirmed in full and free conversations which I sought for with the individual members of your committee. Their statements, as you will perceive, present the subject in a somewhat different aspect from that in which I had considered it, and throw upon me a responsibility which I should be reluctant to assume. They seem to furnish the same reasons in a stronger light for my remaining as your pastor, which had before prevented me from asking you for a discharge.

They place me in a condition in which I could not withdraw from your service without appearing negligent of your wishes and regardless of your welfare. At the same time, they do not convince me that the permanent continuance of my ministry with you would insure even your external prosperity as a society. I am still of the opinion that the service which is desired could be more effectually performed by other hands than mine. I am unwilling, however, to break from you abruptly, to leave you in a state which might terminate in the slightest injury, or to neglect the opportunity of giving a fair trial to the success of my ministry, under the conditions which I shall state. I accordingly consent to comply with the suggestions in the letter of your committee, and to continue the pastoral relation with the distinct understanding that it shall be for a limited period. If at the expiration of one year from this time, or at any earlier date, it should seem that the obstacles to my removal have ceased to exist, I shall then respectfully solicit you to accept the resignation of my office, and I know of nothing but the most resistless conviction that the contrary course would be my duty, that is likely to change this determination. Meantime, I wish to renounce, and I hereby do renounce, all claims upon you for the fulfillment of any pecuniary contract, as I shall consent to receive nothing from the funds of the society which is not a perfectly voluntary contribution on the part of every individual by whom it is paid.

This leads me to speak of another circumstance,

which must always embarrass the relations between minister and people, under our existing arrangements. I mean the inducement for the owner of a pew to continue a member of a religious society after he has lost his interest in the worship. No spir'tual relation can be sincere and efficacious which does not rest on the most perfect freedom. The moment you feel obliged to attend on a religious service, without any inward sympathy, the service can do you no good. There should not be the shade of a restraint on any worshiper, which prevents him from seeking such influences as are most congenial to his tastes, and adapted to his moral and intellectual wants. The minister should feel that the persons whom he addresses have come around him through interest in his words, and whenever that interest ceases they should be able to depart as freely as they came. This would greatly increase the life and animation of our public services. The speaker would have nothing to do but to declare the word which pressed for utterance, and in the manner which his own nature best permitted; the dread of injuring a hearer would never tempt him to modify his thoughts; for no man who heard what was without interest for him would be forced to come a second time. The freedom of the speaker and the freedom of the hearer, which are each equally important, would thus be secured; no man would suffer in his property from the convictions of the preacher; misunderstandings would be ess frequent; and the ties which bound the society together would be of a purer and stronger character than those which now exist.   At present, in all our churches, many are retained by their property in the house, not by their interest in the preacher.   They have heard all he has to say, and it is certainly just that they should have no temptation to continue when they are not edified.

For my own part, I have long been persuaded that we should offer a more spiritual worship, enjoy a more sincere communion with each other, and find our Sabbath services far more attractive and fruitful, were all such restrictions removed, even if we came together as the disciples did, in a large upper room, in a fisher's boat, or by the shore of the sea.   The minister should take his stand where he can freely speak out all that is in his soul.   He would be joined by those who find that he addresses a powerful and living word to their hearts, who are helped by him in their endeavors after a just and truthful life, and are drawn by a spiritual affinity with the message he declares, and who are too desirous that the truth of God should prevail to think of its external, temporary effects.   Such an assembly would constitute the true church of the first-born.   It would consist of those who are united by no other tie than faith in divine things ; by the desire to cultivate the holiest principles of our nature, — reverence, justice, and love ; to ascertain and follow the laws of Providence in the constitution of the inner spirit and of the outward world ; and to convert the jarring elements of earth into materials for a pure, serene, and joyful life.

The basis of worship in such a church would be

6

feeling, not speculation ; the platform would be broad enough to welcome every seeking spirit, in whatever stage of its progress it might be ; all should be encouraged, none should be excluded ; and especially they who are yet feeling after God, if haply they may find him, should be taken by the hand, not driven from the fold. This would leave the investigation of truth entirely free. The sincerest convictions could be uttered without dread or misgiving. We should meet, not as having attained, but as learners ; of course, every ray of light would be sought, not shunned ; we should let the dead past bury its dead ; we should look on life and truth with young eyes ; and thus seeking to be as little children, we should enter the Kingdom of God, and we should know where we were by the divine peace and joy with which our hearts would overflow. In such a church there could be no cold or formal preaching. The instruction would be the overflowing of an individual soul ; there would be no aim at effect. The topics of discourse would be taken from the experience of life ; they would embrace the widest range of thought, and the more exciting and Soul-stirring the better. The infinite Bible of the Universe would be the text-book, and whatever the soul feels or forbodes, the commentary.

But so long as the questions which relate to the highest truth and duty, though discussed everywhere else, are virtually excluded from the pulpit ; so long as the minister is expected to adapt himself to the state of the times, to popular opinion and prevailing prejudices; so long as he is valued more for his plausible and obliging spirit than for his fearless rebuke of sin and detection of error, we may be lulled into treacherous slumber by the services of the church, but they can never accomplish their purpose in arousing the guilty from their sleep of death, pouring light over the darkened mind, and advancing the reign of truth, justice, and love over the kingdoms of men.

This idea of social worship can be carried into effect only in a congregation where there is a prevailing harmony of sentiment between the people and the minister; where the questions which most interest his mind are those which they are also most desirous to hear discussed; where the arrangements of the society allow the most perfect freedom of departure to all who have ceased to be interested in the views that are advanced. Whenever the attention of the minister is strongly drawn to subjects which are not regarded as important by the hearer, the free, sympathetic chain which binds heart with heart is disturbed, no electric spark is drawn forth, the speaker loses his power, and the people are not moved.

Now this is precisely the position which one portion of our community holds towards another, and, in many cases, ministers and people share in its embarrassments. If a minister is stationary and his people are for progress, there is an interruption of sympathy. There is a similar interruption if a people is stationary, while the minister is for progress. And the same is true with regard to any other points on which the community is divided.

The attention of some good men is directed chiefly to individual evils; they wish to improve private character without attacking social principles which obstruct all improvement; while the attention of other good men is directed to the evils of society; they think that private character suffers from public sins, and that, as we are placed in society by Providence, the advancement of society is our principal duty. With regard to these questions there is a great difference of opinion. They compose the principal subjects of thought at the present day. They form what is called the exciting questions by which society is now agitated. I should not do justice, my friends, to you or myself, if I were to close this communication without noticing the ground I have occupied in regard to those questions. It has been made, as you are aware, the cause of some reproach. A popular cry has been started by many individuals against the advocates of new views on philosophy and the condition of society, and, in common with many others, you have heard accusations brought against principles by those who have failed even to explain the meaning of the terms by which they were denounced.

There is a class of persons who desire a reform in the prevailing philosophy of the day. These are called Transcendentalists, because they believe in an order of truths which transcends the sphere of the external senses. Their leading idea is the supremacy of mind over matter. Hence they maintain that the truth of religion does not depend on tradition, nor historical facts, but has an unerring witness in the

soul. There is a light, they believe, which enlight-
eneth every man that cometh into the world ; there
is a faculty in all — the most degraded, the most ignorant, the most obscure — to perceive spiritual truth
when distinctly presented ; and the ultimate appeal
on all moral questions is not to a jury of scholars, a
hierarchy of divines, or the prescriptions of a creed,
but to the common sense of the human race. These
views I have always adopted ; they have been at the
foundation of my preaching from the first time that
I entered the pulpit until now. The experience and
reflection of nearly twenty years have done much
to confirm, nothing to shake, them ; and if my discourses in this house, or my lectures in yonder ves-
try, have in any instance displayed the vitality of
truth, impressed on a single heart a genuine sense of
religion, disclosed to you a new prospect of the resources of your own nature, made you feel more
deeply your responsibility to God, cheered you in
the sublime hope of immortality, and convinced your
reason of the reality and worth of the Christian revelation, it was because my mind has been trained in
the principles of Transcendental Philosophy, — a philosophy which is now taught in every Protestant university on the Continent of Europe, which is the common creed of the most enlightened nations, and the
singular misunderstanding of which among ourselves
illustrates more forcibly, I am ashamed to say, the
heedless enterprise than the literary culture of our
countrymen. If you ask, why I have not preached
the philosophy in the pulpit, I answer that I could not

have preached without it, but my main business as a minister, I conceive, has been, not to preach philosophy or politics or medicine or mathematics, but the Gospel of Christ. If you ask whether I embrace every unintelligible production of the mind that is quoted from mouth to mouth as Transcendentalism, I answer, that if any man writes so as not to be understood, be he Transcendentalist or Materialist, it is his own fault, not another's; for my own part, I agree with Paul, "that I had rather speak five words with my understanding, that by my voice I might teach others also, than ten thousand words in an unknown tongue." There is another class of persons who are devoted to the removal of the abuses that prevail in modern society. They witness the oppressions that are done under the sun, and they cannot keep silence. They have faith that God governs man; they believe in a better future than the past. Their daily prayer is for the coming of the kingdom of righteousness, truth, and love; they look forward to a more pure, more lovely, more divine state of society than was ever realized on earth. With these views, I rejoice to say, I strongly and entirely sympathize. While I do not feel it my duty to unite with any public association for the promotion of these ideas, it is not because I would disavow their principles, but because in many cases the cause of truth is carried forward better by individual testimony than by combined action. I would not be responsible for the measures of a society; I would have no society responsible for me; but in public and private, by

word and by deed, by persuasion and example, I
would endeavor to help the progress of the great
principles which I have at heart. The purpose of
Christianity, as I firmly believe, is to redeem society
as well as the individual from all sin. As a Christian, then, I feel bound to do what I can for the promotion of universal temperance, to persuade men to
abandon every habit which is at war with their physical welfare and their moral improvement, and to produce, by appeals to the reason and conscience, that
love of inward order which is beyond the reach of
legal authority. As a Christian, I would aid in the
overthrow of every form of slavery; I would free
the mind from bondage and the body from chains, I
could not feel that my duty was accomplished while
there was one human being, within the sphere of my
influence, held to unrequited labor at the will of an
other, destitute of the means of education, or doomed
to penury, degradation, and vice by the misfortune of
his birth. I conceive it to be a large share of the
minister's duty to preach the gospel to the poor, to
announce glad tidings of deliverance to all that are
oppressed. His warmest sympathies should be with
those who have none to care for them; he should
never be so much in earnest as when pleading the
cause of the injured. His most frequent visits will
not be to the abodes of fashion and luxury, but to
the dwellings where not many of the wise and mighty
of this world are apt to enter; and if he can enjoy
the poor man's blessing, whom he has treated like an
equal and a brother in all the relations of life, whose

humble abode he has cheered by the expression of honest sympathy, and whose hard lot draws tears from those unused to sorrow, he will count it a richer reward than the applause of society or the admiration of listening crowds. There is another cause in which I feel the strongest interest, and which I would labor to promote, — that of inward peace between man and man. I have no faith whatever in the efficacy or the lawfulness of public or private wars. If they have ever been necessary in the progress of society, as I know they have been unavoidable, it was owing to the prevalence of the rude, untamed animal passions of man over the higher sentiments of his nature. It should be the effort of every true man to abolish them altogether; to banish the principles from which they proceed; to introduce the empire of justice and love; and to abstain on all occasions from the indulgence of bitterness or wrath in his own conduct, and to offer no needless provocation for its indulgence in others. I believe in the omnipotence of kindness, of moral intrepidity, of divine charity. If society performed its whole duty, the dominion of force would yield to the prevalence of love, our prisons would be converted into moral hospitals, the schoolmaster would supersede the executioner, violence would no more be heard in our land, nor destruction in our borders. Our walls would be salvation, and our gates praise.

I have thus laid before you, my friends, what I proposed to communicate on this occasion. I have used great plainness of speech. I have kept nothing back. I have omitted no topic on which I thought light or explanation was demanded. You will have no further occasion to inquire from others what I believe or think, as you have received as explicit disclosures as I know how to make from my own lips. If, after you have heard the statements now presented, you shall arrive at different conclusions from those contained in the letter of your committee; if you shall think that another's voice can be heard here with greater advantage than my own; if you shrink from one who comes before you laden with so many heresies; I shall claim no privilege in this place. I shall consult your truest interests ever; and I cannot believe that they will be promoted by your being compelled to listen to one with whom you feel a diminished sympathy. If, on the other hand, you do not decline my services, on the conditions which I have stated, it will be my earnest endeavor to build you up in holiness, in freedom, in faith, so long as I stand here. But I can never be a different man from what God has made me. I must always speak with frankness the word that comes into my heart; and my only request is that it may be heard with the same frankness and candor with which it is uttered.

One word more and I will stop. The correspondence which has taken place has been spoken of as the sign of a difficulty between the people and minister of this congregation. This is not the case. There is no difficulty, no misunderstanding, in that relation. I have never received greater proofs of confidence, attachment, and esteem, than during this discussion.

I have never felt greater attachment to my friends and brothers here than I do at this moment. If uncalled for words have ever fallen from the lips of any individual or from my own, it is the infirmity or human nature; not, I am sure, the fruit of deliberate unkindness; and as I hope to be forgiven, I forgive everything. Where there is honor and justice and the fear of God on both sides, as I trust there is here, there is seldom any need of the slightest difficulty. What we all desire is the best interests of the society, of the families that worship here, of the souls that look to this place for immortal food. We have been together too long; we have known each other too well; we have stood too often by each other's side in scenes of joy and in the hour of grief, for any unworthy emotion to be cherished long in our breasts. I look on these walls with inexpressible interest; every seat has a story to tell of the past which we cannot think of unmoved. We have sat in heavenly places here with those who are now in heavenly places above; our songs have ascended in pleasant harmony with those who now offer praise before the highest throne; the venerable and the beloved have been trained to holiness in our companionship; whatever may be the future we have been blest in the past; and whether this pulpit shall be filled by him who now addresses you, or by another who shall fill .t more worthily, he will never cease to call down upon it the choicest benedictions of Heaven.

"Peace be within these walls, and prosperity within

this dwelling. For my brethren and companions sake, I will ever say, peace be within thee."

I remain your devoted and affectionate servant,

GEORGE RIPLEY.

BOSTON, *October* 1, 1840.

To a letter like this, — so frank and sincere, betraying in every line so profound a feeling of the incompatibility which existed between minister and people, so fraught with open secrets, — there could be no reassuring answer. The ultimate event was clearly foreseen. On the 1st of January, 1841, the minister addressed a note to the proprietors, requesting to be permitted to depart after three months more of service. On the 31st of the month the proprietors approved a letter accepting the resignation, and resolutions expressing, in terms of unqualified import, confidence and affection. The farewell discourse, a model of dignified speech, gentle, delicate, sympathetic enough, touching, but not dwelling, on the causes of the separation, a truly pastoral sermon, was delivered March 28th, and printed for the use of the church in a pamphlet, which contained, besides the sermon, the communications which recorded the final separation.

Thus the ministry ended, never, in that form, to be resumed. But to the end of his days Mr. Ripley looked back on it with tender interest.

At Brook Farm he enjoyed the singing of the familiar hymn-tunes of the old service. In New York it was his habit, until infirmity prevented, to attend religious worship. He clung to sacred associations; deplored the tendency to make religious observances secular by substituting halls for meeting-houses, and lectures for sermons; and held in high esteem the earnest prophets of the soul. As late as 1875, he wrote to an old Boston friend, a contributor to the " American Cyclopædia ": " You take it for granted that I feel but little interest in the old Unitarianism, which is not the case. I owe it a great debt of gratitude for the best influences that my youth enjoyed; and if any little success has attended my subsequent career, it has been chiefly caused by the impulses I received in Boston, and especially from my association with the liberal and noble minded men whom I loved as friends and honored as guides." In 1879 he wrote in similar strains to Dr. G. W. Hosmer: " I trust that it is not a weakness of advanced years that I cherish so strong an affection for my old Massachusetts friends, and especially for my brethren in the Unitarian ministry, whom I always regard as the best specimens of noble and en lightened manhood that I ever met with."

His last service was rendered at the ordination of his successor, J. I. T. Coolidge, on February 9, 1842, on which occasion he came from Brook Farm to deliver the "Address to the People." The meeting-house was repaired, and, as far as was proper, embellished for the new pastor; but in vain. In less than five years it was thought wise to change the location; the corner-stone of a new, and for that time sumptuous, edifice was laid, May 3, 1847; on the same day, the year following, it was dedicated. The name of the society was changed to the "Thirteenth Congregational Church of the City of Boston;" substantially another society was formed in another part of the town, at the corner of Harrison Avenue and Beach Street; but fortune did not smile on the undertaking. In 1860 the society was dissolved, and at present no longer exists. The very records of the church were lost. A single charred volume of business entries remains to tell the story of financial relations.

CHAPTER II.

GERMS OF THOUGHT.

GEORGE RIPLEY'S literary activity began early, and was from the first directed to the deepest problems. For a short period he edited the "Christian Register," which, in his hands, was all that it was designed to be, an organ of liberal views in theology. His occasionally printed sermons and tracts ever bore upon some interesting phase of speculation. Between 1830 and 1837 he wrote ten articles for the "Christian Examiner," all either stating or foreshadowing his later conclusions. The first paper, on Degerando (September, 1830), indicated the theory of self-education as self-development. The second, "Religion in France" (July, 1831), contains an enthusiastic plea for spiritual Christianity, without priest, dogma, or intellectual limitation. This was followed by "Pestalozzi" (January, 1832), and by a notice of Follen's Inaugural. A paper reviewing Mackintosh's Ethical Philosophy, clear, forcible, argumentative, defends the doctrine of a moral sense in man. To some degree the same

doctrine had come out in the article on Pestalozzi, whose humane aspirations found a hearty
response from the American critic, and whose
experiment, " Neuhof," may have been one of
the incentives to Brook Farm. Next (May,
1835) came a review of Marsh's translation of
Herder. The reviewer speaks with some reserve of German theologians, but praises Tholuck, protests against the indiscriminate charge
of mysticism and obscurity, and repels the no-
tion that German philosophy is irreligious. A
new reformation, he contends, is started in Germany by men like Herder, Baumgarten, Semler, Ernesti, and Michaelis. A characteristic
paper on Herder's theological opinions was also
printed in 1835. In March, 1836, came an article, mainly translated, on Schleiermacher, who,
he thinks, " is without a representative in our
theological progress." The remarkable article
on Martineau's " Rationale of Religious Inquiry " appeared in the " Examiner " for November, 1836. In this paper a distinction is
made between liability to error and absence of
that inspiration, which, in spite of incidental
error, is claimed for the writers of the New Testament, as well as for the prophets and law-giv-
ers of the ancient dispensation, for the soul of
man, but for Christ alone, " in entire and absolute completeness." This article caused great

sensation. Mr. Andrews Norton called atten
tion to it in the " Boston Daily Advertiser,'
condemning its doctrines as leaning toward infidelity, and rebuking the presumption of the
young writer. Mr. Ripley printed a rejoinder
in the same paper on the very next day. This
was the last paper of importance that he sent
to the " Examiner," for the translation from
Ullman of Herder's " Theological Aphorisms "
(January, 1837) contained nothing suggestive.
About this time there was much interest among
Unitarians in new views on Christianity and
Religion. In May of that year Orville Dewey
delivered the Dudleian Lecture at Cambridge,
choosing " Miracles " as his theme. The first
volume of Norton's " Genuineness of the Gospels " was published in 1837, and straightway
reviewed in the " Examiner," by A. A. Liver-
more. James Walker, A. P. Peabody, Orville
Dewey, and other leaders of thought were writing in the " Examiner " about Revelation, Miracles, Inspiration, Christ's Moral Character.
In the " Examiner " for March, 1833, F. H.
Hedge published an article on Coleridge, in
which he found occasion to commend Kant,
Fichte, especially Schelling, and spoke warmly
of the intellectual and spiritual influence of the
transcendental philosophy. This paper was
praised by Mr. Ripley in the " Register," and

was, doubtless, of potent influence in determining the bent of his mind.

The "Discourses on the Philosophy of Religion Addressed to Doubters who wish to Believe," — published in 1836, — comprised six sermons, one of which, the fifth, "On the Coincidence of Christianity with the Higher Nature of Man," had been printed before in the "Liberal Preacher." The little volume was not issued by way of controversy. The professed aim was "the quickening of a pure faith in spiritual truth by a calm exposition of some of the principles on which it rests." The discourses present the positive side of the author's faith. They are in tone sympathetic and gracious, charged with a serene and confiding piety. The "Examiner" speaks of the book as "one of the happiest among the many indications we have had of late of a disposition to introduce a higher tone of spirituality into the preaching of Unitarians." In 1838 appeared the first two volumes of the series entitled "Specimens of Foreign Standard Literature," which extended to fourteen volumes, by J. S. Dwight, Margaret Fuller, C. C. Felton, W. H. Channing, J. F. Clarke, Samuel Osgood, and C. T. Brooks. The "Philosophical Miscellanies," as the opening volumes were called, contained careful introductory and critical notices of the works of Cousin, Jouffroy, and Constant, especially of Cousin, accompanied by translations of such passages from their published writings as were judged best suited to illustrate the course of French philosophy in its pursuit of an ideal aim. These volumes had a marked influence on the educated men of that day, especially in New England. They were afterwards — in 1857 — republished in Edinburgh.

By this time the way was prepared for the vindication of Spinoza, Schleiermacher, and De Wette against the charge of atheism and irreligion brought by Mr. Andrews Norton. Mr. Emerson's famous " Address to the Alumni of the Cambridge Divinity School " was given in 1838. It effectually discharged the electricity that was in the air. At the succeeding anniversary, in 1839, Andrews Norton gave the address on " The Latest Form of Infidelity." It was a resolute, unflinching, scornful, but able and strong attack on the prevailing philosophical tendency. His doctrine was " Sensationalism " of an extreme type.

" To the demand for certainty, let it come from whom it may, I answer, that I know of no bsolute certainty, beyond the limit of momentary consciousness, — a certainty that vanishes the instant it exists, and is lost in the region of metaphysical doubt." " There can be no intui tion, no direct perception, of the truth of Christianity, no metaphysical certainty." "We must use the same faculties and adopt the same rules, in judging concerning the facts of the world which we have not seen, as concerning those of the world of which we have seen a very little." "We proceed throughout upon probabilities." "Of the facts on which religion is founded, we can pretend to no assurance, except that derived from the testimony of God, from the Christian revelation." "We can have no *religious* sentiment of the Infinite, unless we have faith in the one Infinite Being, the God of Christianity. We can have no *religious* love of the beautiful and true, or, in common language, of beauty and truth, if we do not recognize something beautiful and true beyond the limits of this world." "He who has any religious sentiment must have a religious creed." "Religious principle and feeling, however important, are necessarily founded on the belief of certain facts: of the existence and providence of God, and of man's immortality. Now the evidence of these facts is not intuitive." "Our belief in those truths, the evidence of which we cannot examine for ourselves, is founded in a greater or less degree on the testimony of others, who have examined their evidence, and whom we regard as intelligent and trustworthy."

The reply, published anonymously, by "An Alumnus," in 1839, was a model of controversial writing, — clear, calm, impersonal, not free from asperity, but free from bitterness. Theodore Parker said, in a letter to a friend : " Ripley is writing the reply to Mr. Norton. It will make a pamphlet of about one hundred pages octavo, and is clear, strong, and good. He will not say all that I wish might be said ; but, after we have seen that, I will handle, in a letter to you, certain other points not approached by Ripley. There is a higher word to be said on this subject than Ripley is disposed to say just now." The " Alumnus " did indeed, in his first letter, confine himself to the main point raised by Mr. Norton, namely, his adoption and defense of the " Exclusive Principle," in an address before an assembly of liberal clergymen. The doctrine disputed is that the " MIRACLES RECORDED IN THE NEW TESTAMENT ARE THE ONLY PROOF OF THE DIVINE ORIGIN OF CHRISTIANITY." For himself, the writer disclaims historical unbelief.

" The question at issue," he says, " ought to be distinctly understood. It is not concerning the divine mission of Jesus Christ. The certainty of that will be at the foundation of my reasonings, and it is admitted, as far as I know, in all the controversies to which the subject has given rise in our own country.

"Nor is it whether Jesus Christ performed the miracles ascribed to him in the New Testament. I shall hereafter allude to the doubts which are felt by many excellent Christians on this point; but, for my own part, I cannot avoid the conclusion that the miracles related in the Gospels were actually wrought by Jesus. Without being blind to the difficulties of the subject, I receive this view, according to my best knowledge and understanding, on the evidence presented, and in this belief I am joined by a large number of those, against whom your charge of infidelity is alleged, among ourselves.

"Neither does the question I am about to consider relate to any philosophical explanation of the miracles of Christ. I believe that he gave health to the sick, sight to the blind, and life to the dead; and my explanation of these facts is that presented in the New Testament."

The error he combats is opposed on several grounds: 1. As being bold, extravagant, and novel. 2. As being contrary to the clear and express teachings of the Scriptures, both of the Old and the New Testament. 3. As being incompatible with precise directions to scrutinize and reject miraculous claims when put forward by false prophets. 4. The doctrine that miracles are the only evidence of a divine revelation, if generally admitted, would impair the influ-

ence of the Christian ministry, by separating
the pastor of a church from the sympathies of
his people. 5. It would have an injurious bearing on the character of a large portion of the
most sincere believers in Christ. 6. It removes
Christianity from its stronghold in the common
mind, and puts it into the keeping of scholars
and antiquaries. " Christian Truth," it is asserted, "has always been addressed to the ' intuitive perceptions' of the common mind. A
shallow and presumptuous philosophy — presumptuous because shallow — usurps the place
of the simplicity of Christ, and would fain
smother the breathing life of heavenly truth.
Creeds came into the church with the dreams
of speculation. They have been handed down
through the dust of the schools ; they have
sought their principal defense in the subtile,
shadowy, and artificial distinctions of the
learned ; and the most vigorous attacks they
have received have come from the unarmed
strength of plebeian sects."

Mr. Norton put the substance of this Letter
contemptuously aside, as not being addressed
to an examination of his reasoning. He could
hardly say that of the two subsequent Letters,
which were devoted to a defense of Spinoza,
Schleiermacher, and De Wette against the
charge of atheism and irreligion. In the second

of these, page 148, occurs this language: " The principle that the soul has no faculty to perceive spiritual truth is contradicted, I believe, by the universal consciousness of man. God has never left himself without witness in the human heart. The true light has shone, more or less brightly, on every man that cometh into the world. This Divine Spirit has never ceased to strive with the children of earth; it has helped their infirmities, given them just and elevated conceptions, touched their eyes with celestial light, and enabled them to see the beauty and glory of divine things. God has ever manifested himself to his intelligent creatures; but have they no faculty to behold this manifestation? No; man has the faculty for ' feeling and perceiving religious truth.' So far from being imaginary, it is the highest reality of which the pure soul is conscious. Can I be more certain that I am capable of looking out and admiring the forms of external beauty, ' the frail and weary weed in which God dresses the soul that he has called into time,' than that I can also look within, and commune with the fairer forms of truth and holiness, which plead for my love, as visitants from heaven?"

In the second Letter, that on Spinoza, he had written : " They (scholars) are called on for the most gracious sympathies with the whole

community. They should freely give of all the
light which they have freely received. This
cannot be done by diverting public attention
from general topics to personal interests. These
topics must be met with manliness and with
temperate zeal. There must be no disguise, no
timidity, no bitterness, no exclusiveness. Even
those of us who are deeply sensible of having
no claim on the attention of the public, and
who would gladly exchange the field of dispute
'for the still and quiet air of delightful studies,'
or the more attractive walks of practical usefulness, are bound to utter the word which it may
be given us to speak." Then follows a quiet
but unsparing criticism of what he considers
Mr. Norton's unjust aspersions on a "devout,
sweet, unselfish, truth-seeking" man.

This was in 1840. In 1855, noticing in the
New York " Tribune " Mr. Norton's translation of the Gospels, he said of its author : " His
mind was so habitually severe in its action, his
demand for clearness of thought and expression
was so unrelenting, and his opinions were so
accurately formed and so firmly held, that no
production of his pen could fail of bearing the
characteristic stamp of his individual genius
and culture. . . . He often expressed rash and
hasty judgments in regard to the labors of recent or contemporary scholars, consulting his

prejudices, as it would seem, rather than competent authority. But in his own immediate
department of sacred learning he is entitled to
the praise of sobriety of thought and profound-
ness of investigation." Later still, in a chapter
on "Philosophic Thought in Boston," written
for the "Memorial History," the younger oppo-
nent writes thus of his antagonist: "Contemporary with Professor Frisbie, and united with
him by the most intimate ties of friendship and
sympathy, was Andrews Norton, who, though
trained in a different philosophical school, the
principles of 'which he always cherished with
singular tenacity, holds a distinguished place
among the intellectual influences which have
helped to stamp the society of Boston with an
impress of liberal inquiry and original thought
in the sphere of letters, philosophy, and art."
The whole passage is remarkable as a tribute
to an extraordinary man, and as an illustration
of that rare balance of mind, that unfailing
equity and sweetness of temper, which distinguished George Ripley through life.

In the same year that this controversy was
going on (1840), in connection with R. W. Emerson and Margaret Fuller, Mr. Ripley established "The Dial," a monthly magazine for religion, literature, and art, of which he was the
resident editor in Boston until his removal to

Brook Farm in 1841.   During the short period
of his association with it he contributed two
articles, one a review of Orestes A. Brownson's writings, the other a " Letter to a Theological Student."   The first is a hearty tribute
to "a writer whose native force of mind, combined with rare philosophical attainments, has
elevated him to a prominent rank among the
living authors of this country."   The second is
a warm exhortation to a young aspirant after
the honors of the ministry to direct his eyes
earnestly to " the great lights above and within."
He recommends familiar acquaintance with Herder's " Letters on the Study of Theology," and
says: " In Europe a new life has sprung up
from the ashes of a departed faith ; a hag-like,
scholastic theology has given up the ghost, upon
being brought out of darkness into daylight;
and a virgin form appears, radiant with beauty,
and already uttering the same words with which
angel voices heralded the birth of Christ.   It
is for our young men to welcome this glorious
visitant to their bosoms. . . . Let your mind
be filled and consecrated with the heavenly
spirit of Christ; let your youthful energy be
blended with the meekness and gentleness and
wisdom of your Divine Master, and you will
have everything to hope and little to fear."
The man who could write such words was

surely no denier, but a fervent believer rather. He left the ministry himself, not because he had lost faith in it, but because his soul was kindled with zeal for a new, and, as he felt, better method of applying gospel principles to human society. He had become persuaded, after many years of the ablest service he could render, that the work of the ministry was not the work appointed for him. He honored it, but could perform it no longer; and the only way that he knew of showing how truly he held it in honor was to put its precepts into immediate practice by instituting a social order which should correspond to its requirements; by a heroic attempt to bring the new heaven of prophecy down to the old earth of fact. He had always insisted on a Christian life as the only sure test of a Christian faith; now he meant to put into radical practice the lessons of his own pulpit. The ministry was noble, literature was delightful, but duty he considered before all.

CHAPTER III.

BROOK FARM.

THE plunge from the pulpit to Brook **Farm,** though immediate, was not so headlong as is commonly supposed; on the contrary, it was natural, comparatively easy, almost inevitable. At this distance, sharply contrasting the two situations, — the dignity, leisure, elegance, re-spectability of the one, with the democracy, toil, rudeness, unpopularity of the other; the quiet of the library with the tumult of affairs; the pursuit of high philosophy with the study of soils and crops; the works of Kant, Schelling, Cousin, with muck manuals; broadcloth and beaver with overalls and tarpaulin; it seems as if heroism of an exalted kind, not to say a rash enthusiasm, quite unaccountable in a cautious man, must have stimulated so wild an enter-prise. Heroism there certainly was. There was heroism in the brave preacher who, for nearly fifteen years, had proclaimed a gospel which was unwelcome to the staid Unitarian community whereof he was a member. But Brook Farm was simply the logical completion of the pulpit ministration ; a final proof of the preacher's sincerity. Besides all this, it would be a mistake to suppose that the enterprise looked then as chimerical as to some it does now.

It must be remembered that projects of radical social reform were in the air. To quote the language of John Morley : "A great wave of humanity, of benevolence, of desire for improvement, — a great wave of social sentiment, in short, — poured itself among all who had the faculty of large and disinterested thinking." Dr. Pusey and Dr. Newman, representatives of the vital movement in the direction of spiritual supernaturalism, were thinking and writing. Thomas Arnold and F. D. Maurice were trying to broaden the Church of England in the direction of human progress, so that it might embrace heaven and earth, faith and philosophy, creed and criticism. Carlyle was thundering against shams in religion and politics. Dickens was showing up the abuses, cruelties, and iniquities of the established order. Kingsley was stirring the caldron of social discontent. The teaching of George Combe was heralded as an inspiration. Cobden was inaugurating a new era in industrial undertakings. The corn-law agitation was started. John Bright and Daniel O'Connell were busy at their work of destroying monopolies. In France as well as in

England, in fact all over Europe, the seeds were ripening for the great revolt of 1848.

The influence of the new ideas was felt in the United States. The Communist experiment in Brazil was started in 1841; the Hopedale Community in 1842; Robert Owen's enterprise may be said to have reached its highest level in 1826; the writings of Charles Fourier were interpreted here by Albert Brisbane and Horace Greeley, as early as 1842. No fewer than eleven experiments followed Owen's; no fewer than thirty-four were creations of the impetus given, directly or indirectly, by Fourier. The "enthusiasm of humanity" was widespread. We have the testimony of James Martineau to the fact that Dr. Channing, for a time, fell under the fascination of some of the speculative writers that abounded at that time, who held forth the promise of a Golden Age for society; writers like Rousseau, Godwin, Mary Wollstonecraft, the Pantisocratists like Southey and Coleridge, who actually entertained the thought of going to America to plant an ideal society. Similar plans were eagerly discussed among the friends of progress in Boston, — Mr. and Mrs. Ripley being prominent as talkers and sympathetic as listeners. One of the most susceptible and ardent was Mrs. Ripley, a woman of burning enthusiasm, warm feeling, and pas

sionate will. Theodore Parker made the following entry in his journal: "Mrs. Ripley gave
me a tacit rebuke for not shrieking at wrongs,
and spoke of the danger of losing our humanity
in abstractions."

That so strong a feeling, animating com-
manding minds, kindling the circle in which he
was intimate, should have possessed, and even
carried away, a man wearied by the toil, and
disappointed in the results, of a long ministry
which he had for years been feeling was uncongenial, is not surprising. If he could have foreseen the end from the beginning, the hard, incessant, anxious toil, the meagreness of popular
sympathy, the waning of hopes, the final disappointment; if he could have felt the precarious-
ness of the effort, its hopelessness in view of the
existing social order, its ineffectiveness in that
form, as a scheme for regenerating mankind,
he would probably have hesitated longer than
he did, perhaps have withdrawn entirely. But
at that period there seemed little cause for misgiving. The heavenly Jerusalem was in the
clouds, waiting to descend. The believer was
justified in the persuasion that the time for its
appearing had come. The disciples were gathered; the iniquity of the world was full; the
angel had put the trumpet to his lips.

The earliest articles of association are here
given: —

ARTICLES OF ASSOCIATION OF THE SUBSCRIBERS
TO THE BROOK FARM INSTITUTE OF AGRICULT
URE AND EDUCATION.

Articles of Association made and executed this
twenty-ninth day of September, one thousand eight
hundred and forty-one, by and between the several
persons and their assigns, who have given their sig-
natures to this instrument and by it associated themselves together for the purpose and objects herein-
after set forth : —

ART. I. The name and style of this Association
shall be The Subscribers to the Brook Farm Institute of Agriculture and Education ; and all persons
who shall hold one or more shares of the stock of the
Association shall be members ; and every member
shall be entitled to one vote on all matters relating to
the funds of the Association.

ART. II. The object of the Association is to purchase such estates as may be required for the establishment and continuance of an agricultural, literary,
and scientific school or college, to provide such lands
and houses, animals, libraries and apparatus, as may
be found expedient or advantageous to the main purpose of the Association.

ART. III. The whole property of the Association,
real and personal, shall be vested in and held by Four
Trustees to be elected annually by the Association.

ART. IV. No shareholder shall be liable to any
assessment whatever on the shares held by him, nor
shall he be held responsible individually in his private

property on account of this Association ; nor shall the Trustees, or any officer or agent of the Association, have any authority to do anything which shall impose personal responsibility on any shareholder by making any contracts or incurring any debts for which the shareholders shall be individually or personally responsible.

ART. V. All conveyances to be taken for lands or other real estate purchased by the Association in pursuance of these articles shall be made to the Trustees, their successors in office or survivors as joint tenants, and not as tenants in common.

ART. VI. The Association guarantees to each shareholder the interest of five per cent. annually on the amount of stock held by him in the Association, and this interest may be paid in certificates of stock and credited on the books of the Association ; provided, however, that each shareholder may, at the time of the annual settlement, draw on the funds of the Association, not otherwise appropriated, to an amount not exceeding that of the interest credited in his favor.

ART. VII. The shareholders on their part, for themselves, their heirs and assigns, do renounce all claim on any profits accruing to the Association for the use of their capital invested in the stock of the Association, except five per cent. interest on the amount of stock held by them, payable in the manner described in the preceding article.

ART. VIII. Every subscriber may receive the tuition of one pupil for every share held by him, instead

8

of five per cent. interest, as stated above, or tuition to an amount not exceeding twenty per cent. interest on his investment.

ART. IX. No share shall be transferred from one person to another without the consent of the Trustees, nor shall any such transfer be valid without their signature.

ART. X. Every shareholder may withdraw his amount of stock and whatever interest is due thereon, by giving twelve months' notice to the Trustees of the Association.

ART. XI. The capital stock of the Association, now consisting of Twelve Thousand Dollars, shall be divided into shares of Five Hundred Dollars each, and may be increased to any amount at the pleasure of the Association.

ART. XII. These articles, it is understood and agreed on, are intended for the safe, legal, and orderly holding and management of such property real and personal as shall further the purposes of the " Brook Farm Institute of Agriculture and Education," to which Institute this Association of subscribers is subordinate and auxiliary.

SUBSCRIPTION.

We, the undersigned, do hereby agree to pay the sum attached to our names, to be invested in the Brook Farm Institute of Agriculture and Education, according to the conditions described in the foregoing Articles of Association.

Date, 1841.

NAMES.	SHARES.	SUMS.
Geo. Ripley . . .	No. 1, 2, and 3	$1,500
Nath. Hawthorne .	" 18 and 19	1,000
Minot Pratt . . .	" 4, 5, and 6	1,500
Charles A. Dana .	" 10, 11, and 12 . . .	1,500
William B. Allen .	" 7, 8, and 9	1,500
Sophia W. Ripley .	" 16 and 17	1,000
Maria T. Pratt . .	" 20 and 21	1,000
Sarah F. Stearns .	" 22 and 23	1,000
Marianne Ripley .	" 13, 14, and 15 . . .	1,500
Charles O. Whitmore	" 24	500

OFFICERS.

At a meeting of the Brook Farm Institute of Agriculture and Education, held on Wednesday, September 29, 1841, the following persons were appointed to office as follows : —

General Direction.

Geo. Ripley,　　　　　Minot Pratt,
Wm. B. Allen.

Direction of Finance.

Nath. Hawthorne,　　　Chas. A. Dana,
Wm. B. Allen.

Direction of Agriculture.

Wm. B. Allen,　　　　Minot Pratt,
Geo. Ripley.

Direction of Education.

Sophia W. Ripley,　　　Charles A. Dana,
Marianne Ripley.

Charles A. Dana was appointed Recording Secretary, and Minot Pratt, Treasurer; and the meeting adjourned.

CHAS. ANDERSON DANA, *Secretary.*

At a meeting of the Brook Farm Institute of Agriculture and Education on Saturday last, October 30, ˙41, the following votes were passed : —

Voted, 1. To transfer the Institution recently carried on by George Ripley to the Brook Farm Institute of Agriculture and Education from and after November 1, 1841, according to the conditions stated in the instrument of this date, and signed by George Ripley, William B. Allen, and Charles A. Dana.

2. To transfer the establishment recently carried on by Marianne Ripley to the Brook Farm Institute, from and after November 1, 1841, according to the conditions stated in the instrument referred to in the above vote.

3. That, in the annual settlement with individual members, each member shall be allowed board in proportion to the time employed for the Association : that is, one year's board for one year's labor ; one half year's board for one half year's labor ; and if no labor is done, the whole board shall be charged.

4. That the price of board charged to the Associates shall be $4.00 per week, until otherwise ordered, including house-rent, fuel, light, and washing.

5. That three hundred days' labor shall be considered equal to one year's labor, and shall entitle a person to one share of the annual dividend, and no allowance shall be made for a greater amount of labor.

6. That sixty hours shall be considered equal to

six days' labcr for the months of May, June, July, August, September, and October, inclusive; forty-eight hours, from November to April, inclusive.

7. That for children of the associates, over ten years of age, board shall be charged at half the established rate.

8. That the price of board and tuition shall be $4.00 a week for boys, and $5.00 a week for girls over twelve years of age ; and $3.50 a week for children under that age, exclusive of washing and separate fire.   CHAS. ANDERSON DANA, *Secretary.*

The " Brook Farm Association for Education and Agriculture," was put in motion in the spring of 1841. There was no difficulty in collecting a company of men and women large enough to make a beginning. One third of the subscriptions was actually paid in, Mr. Ripley pledging his library for four hundred dollars of his amount. With the sum subscribed a farm of a little less than two hundred acres was bought for ten thousand five hundred dollars, in West Roxbury, about nine miles from Boston. The site was a pleasant one, not far from Theodore Parker's meeting-house in Spring Street, and in close vicinity to some of the most wealthy, capable, and zealous friends of the enterprise. It was charmingly diversified with hill and hollow, meadow and upland. It possessed, moreover, historical associations, which

were interesting to its new occupants. Here
the "apostle" Eliot preached to the Indians
his grave was hard by. The birth-place was
not far distant of General Warren, of Revolu-
tionary fame. The spot seemed peculiarly appropriate to the uses it was now set apart for.
Later experience showed its unfitness for lucrative tillage, but for an institute of education,
a semi-æsthetic, humane undertaking, nothing
could be better.

This is the place to say, once for all, with the
utmost possible emphasis, that Brook Farm was
not a "community" in the usual sense of the
term. There was no element of "socialism"
in it. There was about it no savor of antino-
mianism, no taint of pessimism, no aroma, however faint, of nihilism. It was wholly unlike
any of the "religious" associations which had
been established in generations before, or any
of the atheistic or mechanical arrangements
which were attempted simultaneously or afterwards. Dr. Channing had said, in a letter to
Rev. Adin Ballou, dated February 27, 1841,
two months before the beginning of Brook
Farm, "I have for a very long time dreamed
of an association in which the members, instead
of preying on one another, and seeking to put
one another down, after the fashion of this
world, should live together as brothers, seeking
one another's elevation and spiritual growth"

The institution of Brook Farm, though far from being "religious" in the usual sense of the word, was enthusiastically religious in spirit and purpose. The faith in the divinity of natural impulse may have been excessive, but emphasis was so strongly laid on the divinity that the common dangers of following impulse were avoided. Confidence in freedom may have been exaggerated, but, inasmuch as the freedom was interpreted as freedom to become wise and good, simple and self-sacrificing, gentle and kind, its earthward tendency was no cause of anxiety. There was no theological creed, no ecclesiastical form, no inquisition into opinions, no avowed reliance on superhuman aid. The thoughts of all were heartily respected; and while some listened with sympathy to Theodore Parker, others went to church nowhere, or sought the privileges of their own communion. At the funeral of one who died in the Episcopal faith, the services were conducted in accordance with that ritual. There were many Swedenborgians in the company; in fact, there was a decided leaning towards the views of the Swedish mystic; but no attempt was made to fashion opinion in that or in any other mould. The spirit of hope in the Association was too elevated for that. It has been well said that the aim of the Association was practical, not theoretical, **not**

transcendental, not intellectual; in the same
breath it must be added that it was, in a high
sense, spiritual; that it was practical because it
was spiritual; that while it aimed at the physical and mental elevation of the poorer classes,
it did so because it believed in their natural capacity for elevation as children of God. The
leaders trusted in the power of light and love,
in natural truth and justice, and were persuaded
that the world could be helped by nothing else.
They believed, therefore they toiled.

More than this, they felt themselves to be
Christians. The name of Jesus was always
spoken with earnest reverence. Mr. W. H.
Channing, then as now an enthusiastic preacher
of gospel righteousness, was a welcome prophet
among them. Their discussions were always
within the limits of the Christian dispensation,
never conducted in the interest of denial or
skepticism. In a word, the faith in mental
freedom was so cordial, sincere, hospitable, that
no intrusion of the sectarian temper was possible; and the persuasion was so clear that the
various forms of religious faith were but so
many adaptations to spiritual need, that none
were tempted to do more than set forth the attractions of their own favorite worship.

In an article written for the " Democratic Review " of November, 1842, the editor, Orestes

A. Brownson, defined Brook Farm as an Industrial Establishment, quoting its founder to that effect. After giving the " clerical " answer to the social problem, the "ethical" answer, the answer of the " politician," the " political economist," the " socialist," Mr. Brownson declares his preference for Brook Farm, as being simple, unpretending, and presenting itself " by no means as a grand scheme of world reform, or of social organization." He describes their leader as " a man of rare attainments, one of our best scholars, as a metaphysician second to no one in the country, and says : "A few men and women, of like views and feelings, grouped themselves around him, not as their master, but as their friend and brother." They " leave the State and Church standing in all their necessity and force." " It essentially breaks the family caste, while it preserves the family inviolate." " Individual property is recognized and sacred. But, by making time, not skill nor intensity, the basis according to which the compensation of labor is determined, and by eating at a common table, and laboring in common and sharing in common the advantages of the individual excellence there may be in the community, the individual feeling is subdued, and, while suffered to remain as a spring of industry, it is shorn of its power to encroach on the social body." The letter printed along with the article — the occasion, in fact, of its being written — dwells on the Christian democracy of the establishment, the good-will, the admirable teaching, the cheerful toil, the happiness of the children, the serviceableness of the women, the diligence in farm, garden, and fruit culture, the cordial humanity, the glad self-sacrifice, the extraordinary combination of religious exaltation with æsthetic taste.

A sympathizing critic published in the "Dial (January, 1842) an account of the enterprise as it then appeared : —

The attempt is made on a very small scale. A few individuals who, unknown to each other, under different disciplines of life, reacting from different social evils, but aiming at the same object, — of being wholly true to their natures as men and women, — have been made acquainted with one another, and have determined to become the faculty of the embryo university.

In order to live a religious and moral life worthy the name, they feel it is necessary to come out in some degree from the world, and to form themselves into a community of property, so far as to exclude competition and the ordinary rules of trade; while they reserve sufficient private property, or the means of obtaining it, for all purposes of independence and isolation at will. They have bought a farm in order to make agriculture the basis of their life, it being the most direct and simple in relation to nature. A true life, although it aims beyond the highest star, is redolent of the healthy earth. The perfume of clover lingers about it. The lowing of cattle is the natural bass to the melody of human voices.

The plan of the Community, as an economy, is, in brief, this : for all who have property to take stock, and receive a fixed interest thereon ; then to keep house or board in common, as they shall severally desire, at the cost of provisions purchased at wholesale, or raised on the farm ; and for all to labor in community and be paid at a certain rate an hour, choosing their own number of hours and their own kind of work. With the results of this labor and their interest they are to pay their board, and also purchase whatever else they require, at cost, at the warehouses of the community, which are to be filled by the community as such. To perfect this economy, in the course of time they must have all trades and all modes of business carried on among themselves, from the lowest mechanical trade which contributes to the health and comfort of life, to the finest art which adorns it with food or drapery for the mind. All labor, whether bodily or intellectual, is to be paid at the same rate of wages, on the principle that, as the labor becomes merely bodily, it is a greater sacrifice to the individual laborer to give his time to it ; because time is desirable for the cultivation of the intellect, in exact proportion to ignorance.

Besides, intellectual labor involves in itself higher pleasures, and is more its own reward, than bodily abor. Another reason for setting the same pecuniary value on every kind of labor is to give outward expression to the great truth that all labor is sacred when done for a common interest. Saints and philosophers already know this, but the childish world does not; and very decided measures must be taken to equalize labor in the eyes of the young of the community, who are not beyond the moral influences of the world without them. The community will have nothing done within its precincts but what is done by its own members, who stand all in social equality: that the children may not " learn to expect one kind of service from Love and Goodwill, another from the obligation of others to render it," a grievance of the common society, stated by one of the associated mothers as destructive of the soul's simplicity. Consequently, as the Universal Education will involve all kinds of operations necessary to the comforts and elegances of life, every associate, even if he be the digger of a ditch as his highest accomplishment, will be an instructor in that to the young members.

Nor will this elevation of bodily labor be liable to lower the tone of manners and refinement in the community. The " children of light " are not altogether unwise in their generation. They have an invisible but all-powerful guard of principles. Minds incapable of refinement will not be attracted into this association. It is an Ideal Community, and only to the 'deally inclined will it be attractive ; but these are to be found in every rank of life, under every shadow of circumstance. Even among the diggers of the ditch are to be found some who, through religious cultivation, can look down in meek superiority upon the outwardly refined and the book learned.

Besides, after becoming members of this community, none will be engaged merely in bodily labor. The hours of labor for the association will be limited by a general law, and can be curtailed at the will of the individual still more ; and means will be given to all for intellectual improvement, and for social intercourse calculated to refine and expand. The hours redeemed from labor by community will not be reapplied to the acquisition of wealth, but to the production of intellectual good. This community aims to be rich, not in the metallic representation of wealth, but in the wealth itself, which money should represent, namely, *leisure to live in all the faculties of the soul.* As a community, it will traffic with the world at large in the products of agricultural labor ; and it will sell education to as many young persons as can be domesticated in the families, and enter into the common life with their own children. In the end it hopes to be enabled to provide not only all the necessaries, but all the elegances desirable for bodily and for spiritual health : books, apparatus, collections for science, works of art, means of beautiful amusement. These things are to be common to all ; and thus that object, which alone gilds and refines the passion for individual accumulation will no longer exist for desire, and, whenever the sordid passion appears, it will be seen in its naked selfishness. In its ultimate success the community will realize all the ends which selfishness seeks, but involved in spiritual blessings which only greatness of soul can aspire after. And the requisitions on the individuals, it is believed, will make this the order forever. The spiritual good will always be the condition of the temporal.

Every one must labor for the community, in a reasonable degree, or not taste its benefits. The principles of the organization, therefore, and not its probable results in future time, will determine its members. These principles are coöperation in social matters, instead of competition or balance of interests; and individual self-unfolding, in the faith that the whole soul of humanity is in each man and woman. The former is the application of the love of man, the latter of the love of God, to life. Whoever is satisfied with society as it is, whose sense of justice is not wounded by its common action, institutions, spirit of commerce, has no business with this community; neither has any one who is willing to have other men (needing more time for intellectual cultivation than himself) give their best hours and strength to bodily labor, to secure himself immunity therefrom. And whoever does not measure what society owes to its members, of cherishing and instruction, by the needs of the individuals that compose it, has no lot in this new society. Whoever is willing to receive from his fellow-men that for which he gives no equivalent will stay away from its precincts forever.

From this extract it will be seen that the in

terests of the higher education, the cultivation
of mind and soul, lay very near the heart of
the noble founder of Brook Farm. He himself
said: "We are a company of teachers. The
branch of industry which we pursue as our
primary object and chief means of support is
teaching." [1]

In regard to individual teachers, it is enough
to say that Mr. Ripley himself taught Intellectual and Moral Philosophy and Mathematics;
Mrs. Ripley was instructor in History and Modern Languages; George P. Bradford took the
department of Belles Lettres; Charles A. Dana
had classes in Greek and German; John S.
Dwight imparted knowledge in Latin and Music; others were employed in the primary and
infant schools. There was an instructor in
Drawing; a teacher also in theoretical and practical Agriculture. Such time as was not occupied in teaching might be devoted to such pursuits as inclination suggested, — farming, gar-
dening, the cultivation of trees, fruits, flowers,
or some branch of domestic service. There was
always enough to do. Mr. Ripley liked to milk
cows, saying that such occupation was eminently
favorable to contemplation, *particularly when
the cow's tail was looped up behind.* He would
also go out in the early morning and help clean
the stable, a foul and severe task, which, it may

[1] See Appendix.

be presumed, he undertook by way of illustrating the principle of self-sacrifice which was at the basis of the experiment.   His wife worked in the laundry until the necessity of economizing strength compelled her to resort to lighter labor, in which her natural elegance and refinement of judgment were required.   When convenient, the men did women's work; the "General," for example, made all the bread and cake and some of the pastry.   On occasion chiefs — if such a term may be allowed — acted as waiters at table.   Everybody was ready for any needed or available service.   The place was a bee-hive.   The head-farmer was hired, most of the members being literary men, unacquainted with the needs of the soil; but, as a rule, the work was done by members.

The establishment of the school was immediate.   In two years the number of scholars was about thirty in a community of seventy. The original pioneers numbered about twenty. There were never more than one hundred and fifty.   The teaching was of a high order, not so much by reason of the accomplishment of the instructors, as in consequence of the singular enthusiasm which animated all concerned in it. pupils no less than preceptors.   Especially in music was the standard of taste exacting whatever may be said of the attainment.   The boys and girls at Brook Farm were familiar with the compositions of Haydn, Mozart, Beethoven, Mendelssohn, Schubert, before the initiation began elsewhere. There was a genuine passion for improvement in intellectual arts, a thirst for knowledge, a hunger for mental stimulus of a powerful kind. When Margaret Fuller visited the institution, and gave one of her eloquent, oracular talks, the interest caught up old and young. Miss Fuller visited Brook Farm, but did not live there; neither did Emerson; neither did W. H. Channing; neither did Theodore Parker; neither did C. P. Cranch, though all came more or less often, and manifested a sincere interest. Many eminent persons came as observers of the experiment, — Orestes A. Brownson, James Walker, Bronson Alcott, and others of less note. The undertaking was so interesting that few people who had at heart the condition of society remained wholly aloof from it. The public curiosity was insatiable. During one year more than four thousand visitors came. Every fine day brought a crowd. The multitude became occasionally an incumbrance. The time of the members was uncomfortably encroached on; their occupations were disturbed. It became necessary at last to charge a small fee for their entertainment in case they required lunch or dinner. Among the callers.

9

to show how miscellaneous were their motives, was the notorious Mike Walsh, who, it is safe to say, was not attracted by any interest in the higher problems of society. The experiment was on too small a scale to engage the attention of deeply theoretical minds, or to be widely significant. Charles Nordhoff, in his history of communistic societies in the United States, makes no mention of Brook Farm. But the eminence of its founder, the high aims of his associates, the well-known sympathy of several distinguished people, the prevalence throughout the community of views similar, at least, to those which animated the association, exerted an influence far beyond its actual domain. It was the earthly base of a celestial idea ; a house in the clouds ; a " castle in Spain " ; none the less but rather so much the more, a castle, for having its towers in the sky.

The applications for admission were numerous, and, for the most part, from people who quite mistook the object the founders had in view. The well-to-do people of the world, the contented, the comfortable, the ambitious, the successful who had attained, the energetic who hoped to attain, the large class of unthinking, conventional people, young or old, rich or poor, educated or uneducated, had no concern with and never came near the institution. To them it was a utopia, visionary, chimerical, notional absurd, a butt for ridicule. But the hungry of heart, the democratic, the aspiring, the sentimental, the poor in spirit or in purse, those who sought a refuge or a place of rest; in some instances those who desired an easy, unlaborious, irresponsible life, knocked for admission at the door. The nature of these overtures can readily be fancied by those who may be a little acquainted with the working of philanthropic establishments; but for the benefit of such as may need enlightenment on this point, a few letters are here inserted with one of Mr. Ripley's replies: —

MASS., *October* 12, 1844.

DEAR SIR, — I take the liberty of inquiring of you whether you can admit into your fraternity a literary old man, aged fifty-four years, who may be able to work perhaps six, eight, or ten hours per day. The work must be, at least at first, somewhat light, as he has never been used to any kind of manual labor. Of late years his attention has been so much devoted to association and peace that he is fit for but little, if any, of the common business of the world, out of an association. He will bring no money, no funds whatever, and no influence into your community. He only desires to be and live and work and coöperate with others; where he can do as he would be done by, and contribute his feeble example in favor of a better order of society than our present antagunistical selfishism.

By giving me such information per mail as you may deem expedient, you will oblige, sir,

Your obedient servant.

June 1, 1843.

DEAR SIR, — I have an earnest and well-matured desire to join your community with my family, if I can do it under satisfactory circumstances, — I mean satisfactory to all parties. I am pastor of the First Congregational Church in this town. My congregation is quiet, and in many respects very pleasant; but I have felt that my views of late are not sufficiently in accordance with the forms under which I have undertaken to conduct the ministry of Christian truth. This want of accordance increases, and I feel that a crisis is at hand. I must follow the light that guides me, or renounce it to become false and dead. The latter I cannot do. I have thought of joining your association ever since its commencement. Is it possible for me to do so under satisfactory circumstances?

I have deep, and I believe intelligent sympathy with your idea. I have a wife and four children, the oldest ten, the youngest seven years old. Our habits of life are very simple, very independent of slavery to the common forms of " gigmanity," and our bodies have not been made to waste and pine by the fashionable follies of this generation. It is our creed that life is greater than all forms, and that the soul's life s diviner than the *conveniences* of fashion.

As to property we can bring you little more than

ourselves. But we can bring a hearty good-will to work, and in work we have some skill. I have un-impaired health, and an amount of muscular strength, beyond what ordinarily falls to the lot of mortals. In the early part of my life I labored on a farm, filling up my leisure time with study, until I entered my present profession. My *hands* have some skill for many things; and if I join you I wish to live a true life. My selfish aims are two: first, I wish to be under circumstances where I may live truly; and second and chiefly I wish to do the best thing for my children.

Be so good as to reply to this at your earliest con-venience. Yours, sincerely. ———

WATERTOWN, *February* 4, 1843.

MESSRS. OF THE COMMUNITY AT WEST ROX-BURY, — I am induced to address you partly at the request of several gentlemen who have formed an association in this place for the purpose of inquiring into the principles of *Fourier's plan* for meliorating the condition of the human race, and also from an intense anxiety on my own part to know the practi-cal working of the plan which you have adopted in your community, and which is said in the public pa-pers to resemble, if not exactly to carry out in detail, the one recommended by the above mentioned writer.

If you will have the goodness to answer the fol-lowing interrogatories, you will not only confer a favor on myself and those gentlemen who are now investigating this subject in this place, but, by giving such information as is the result of your experience, I trust you will aid the cause of the poor and oppressed, and be instrumental in mitigating the miseries and afflictions of all conditions and classes of men : How long since you first organized your society ? How many associates were there at first ? What was the average amount in money or property that each one contributed to commence with ? Of how many acres does your farm consist ? What was the cost per acre and the terms of payment ? If purchased on time, have you been able, from the proceeds of your farm and other products of your own industry, to sustain the society and meet the payments as they became due ? What is the present number of persons in your association, and in what ratio have they increased ? Do you have many applications for admission, and what are the qualifications requisite for an associate, either in a moral, intellectual, or pecuniary point of view ? In the present state of things, do you think it necessary to success that such a community as yours should be located near a large town or city ? Have any become dissatisfied and withdrawn from your community, and, in case they do leave, are they allowed to take the capital they invested and their earnings ? According to your regulations, can you expel a member ? Have you a written constitution, and, if so, what are its most prominent features ? Does each member choose his or her employment, and work at it when they please ? Have you any particular system for educating the children who belong to your community ? Do you intend to give them what is generally termed a classical education? Have you a common fund, and, if so, how is it raised, and how are the persons chosen who control it? Do you all eat at a common table, and, if so, could a family or an individual, if they preferred it, have their meals in apartments by themselves? Do you think a sufficient time has elapsed since the formation of your society for you or others to judge tolerably correctly of the utility of such associations, by your experiment?

Gentlemen, we can, of course, expect only brief answers to these inquiries; but we trust you will do us the justice to believe that we are actuated by no idle curiosity in thus seeking information.

UTICA, *January* 18, 1844.

SIR, — I have the happiness of being acquainted with a lady who has some knowledge of you, from whose representations I am encouraged to hope that you will not only excuse the liberty I (being a stranger) thus take in addressing you, but will also kindly answer a number of questions I am desirous of being informed upon, relative to the society for social reform to which you belong.

I have a daughter (having five children), who with her husband much wish to join a society of this kind: they have had thoughts of engaging with a society now forming in Rochester, but their friends advise them to go to one that has been some time in operation, because those connected with it will be able to speak with certainty as to whether the working of the system in any way realizes the theory.

1. The first question I would put is, Have you room in your association to admit the above family?

2. And if so, upon what terms would they be received?

3. Would a piano-forte, which two years ago cost $350, be taken at its present value in payment for shares?

4. Would any household furniture be taken in the same way?

5. Do you carry out M. Fourier's idea of diversity of employment?

6. How many members have you at this time?

7. Do the people, generally speaking, appear happy?

8. Would a young man, a mechanic, of unexceptional character, be received, having no capital?

9. Does the system work well with the children?

10. Have you not more than one church, and, if so, what are its tenets?

11. Have parties opportunities of enjoying any other religion?

12. What number of hours are generally employed in labor?

13. What chance for study?

14. Do you meet with society suitable to *your taste?*

Although my questions are so numerous that I fear tiring you, yet I still feel that I may have omitted some inquiry of importance. If so, will you do me the favor to supply the deficiency?

Please to answer my questions by number, as they

are put. · Hoping you will write as soon **as possible**
I **re**main yours respectfully.

BOSTON, *Feb. the* **13. 1844.**

SUR, — As I have hurd something About the sade
broofarm, I thairfore take the Pleasure of wrighting
A fue lines to you dear sur, to inform you sur of my
mind about the sade place. I think sur that I should
like to joine you boath in hart and hand. I am now
stopping at the united states hotell boston. thair is
one Mr. thomas Whitch is going with you in Apr.
next he is a friend of mine I. think I. would like
to go with him if I. could I. am tiard of liveing in
the city I. would like to change my life if I. could
be of any service to you in brookfarm I. think I. d
like to Join you and do all in my power to premote
the cause. I. would like to know the rules of the
community if you sur Wright a fue lines to me and
direct them to the united states hotell I. would be
very happy to recive. indeed I. think I. would like
to work on the farm this summer I should like to
know what I should be alowed the first year. I.
would like to lurn some trade in the winter. I. am
single my age is 19. my name —— I hope sur that
you may soon wright me a letter Whare I. may have
the pleashure of seeing you soon. I. have more to
say sur when I see you. I. would like to see you
this week if possible. F. F. C., Boston.

I will try to come out with my friend in the course
of a week or two if I. do not see you before. but
please wright me a letter if I do not see you.

Boston, *March* 1, 1844.

MR. GEORGE RIPLEY, *Pres. of the west roxbry association:*

as I wish to goin your society and not knoing the termes on wich members are admited I wish to be informed and the amount wich must be paid in. thare is six in the famely and as I am poor I wish to know the least sum wich we can be admited for. if you will pleaze to write and inform mee of the perticulars you will oblige your humble servent,

July 13, 1845.

DEAR SIR, — Will you step aside for a moment from the many duties, the interesting cares, and soul-stirring pleasures of your enviable situation and read a few lines from a stranger? They come to you not from the cold and sterile regions of the north, nor from the luxuriant, yet untamed wilds of the west, but from the bright and sunny land where cotton flowers bloom; where nature has placed her signet of beauty and fertility. Yes, sir, the science that the immortal Fourier brought to light has reached the far south, and I trust has warmed many hearts and interested many minds; but of one alone will I write. It is to *me* a dawn of a brighter day than has ever yet risen upon the world — a day when man shall be redeemed from his more than "Egyptian bondage," and stand erect in moral, intellectual, and physical beauty. I have lived forty years in the world, and divided that time between the Eastern, Middle, and Southern States; have seen life as exhibited in city and country ; have mingled with the most intelligent and with the unlettered rustic ; have marked society in a variety of phases, and find amid all that selfishness has warped the judgment, chilled the affections, and blunted all the fine feelings of the soul. I am weary and worn with the heartless folly, the wicked vanity, and shameless iniquity which the civilized world everywhere presents. Long have I sighed for something higher, nobler, holier than aught found in this world ; and have sometimes longed to lay my body down where the weary rest, that my spirit might dwell in perfect harmony. But since the beautiful science of amity has dawned upon my mind, my heart has loved to cherish the bright anticipations of hope, and I see in the dim distance the realization of all my wishes. I see a generation coming on the arena of action, bearing on their brows the impress of their noble origin, and cultivating in their hearts the pure and exalted feelings that should ever distinguish those who bear the image of their Maker. Association is destined to do much for poor suffering humanity : to elevate, refine, redeem the race and restore the purity and love that made the bowers of Eden so surpassingly beautiful.

You, sir, and your associates are pioneers in a noble reform. May the blessing of God attend you. I am anxious to be with you for various reasons. The first is, I have two little daughters whom I wish to bring up amid healthful influences, with healthy and untrammeled bodies, pure minds, and all their young affections and sympathies clustering around their hearts. I never wish their minds to be under the influence of the god of this generation — fashion; nor their hearts to become callous to the sufferings of their fellows. I never wish them to regard labor as degrading, nor poverty as a crime. Situated as I am I cannot rear them in health and purity, and therefore I am anxious to remove them from the baneful influences that surround them. I look upon labor as a blessing, and feel that every man and woman should spend some portion of each day in healthful employment. It is absolutely necessary to my health, and is also a source of enjoyment even in isolation; how much would that pleasure be increased could I have several kindred spirits around me with whom I could interchange thoughts, and whose feelings and desires flow in the same channel as my own.

Oh, sir, I must live, labor, and *die* in association. Again my heart is pained with the woes of my fellows; with the distressing poverty and excessive labor which are bearing to the grave a portion of the human family. Gladly would I bear my part in raising them to a higher and happier condition; and how can I better do this than by uniting myself with the noble reformers of Brook Farm, where caste is thrown aside and rich and poor constitute but one family. I have not a large fortune, but sufficient to live comfortably anywhere. A large part of it is now vested in houses and lands in Georgia. Such is the low price of cotton that real estate cannot be sold at this time without a ruinous sacrifice. Most of my Georgia property rents for more than the interest of its cost at eight per cent. I have also houses and lands in this state, but cannot for the above-named reasons find a purchaser. Therefore if I go to the Association I shall be obliged to leave some of my possessions unsold, and be content to receive the rent until I can effect a sale. I have no negroes, thank God. Now if you are not full at Brook Farm, and do not object to myself, wife, and two daughters, one four years, the other six months old — presenting ourselves as candidates for admission, and $2,500 or $3,000 will be sufficient for an initiation fee, I shall, as soon as I can arrange my affairs, be with you. I will thank you to write me, informing me with how much ready cash, with an income of $500 or $600 per year, I can be received. Mrs. —— and myself will wish to engage daily in labor. We both labored in our youth ; we wish to resume it again.

Dear Friends, if I may so call you. I read in the " New York Tribune " a piece taken from the " Dial," headed the West Roxbury Community. Now what I want to know is, can I and my children be admitted into your society, and be better off than we are here ? I have enough of the plainest kind to eat and wear here. I have no home but what we hire from year to year. I have no property but movables, and not a cent to spare when the year comes round. I have three children : two boys and a girl ; the oldest fourteen, the youngest nine ; now I want to educate them — how to do it where there is no chance but ordinary schools, — to move into the village, I could not bring the year round, and the danger they would be exposed to without a father to restrain their wanderings would be undertaking more than I dare attempt. Now, if you should presume to let me come, where can I live? Can our industry and economy clothe and feed us for the year? Can I keep a cow? How can I be supplied with fire in that dear place, how can I pay my school bills, and how can I find all the necessary requisites for my children to advance in learning? If I should wish to leave in two, three, or five years, could I and mine, if I paid my way whilst there? If you should let me come, and I should think best to go, *how shall I get there*, what would be my best and cheapest route, how should I proceed with what I have here — sell all off or bring a part? I have three beds and bedding, one cow, and ordinary things enough to keep house. My children are called tolerable scholars; my daughter is the youngest. The neighbors call her an uninteresting child. I have no pretensions to make; my only object is to enjoy the good of the society, and have my children educated and accomplished.

Am I to send my boys off to work alone, or will they have a kind friend to say, Come, boys; and teach them how in love and good will, and relieve me of this heavy task of bringing up boys with nothing to do it with? If your religion has a name I should like well enough to know it; if not, and the substance is love to God and good will to man, my mind is well enough satisfied. I have reflected upon this subject ever since I read the article alluded to, and now I want you to write me every particular. Then, if you and I think best in the spring, I will come to you. We are none of us what can be called weakly. I am forty-six years old, able to do as much every day as to spin what is called a day's work. Not that I expect you spin much there, only that is the amount of my strength as it now holds out. I should wish to seek intelligence, which, as you must know, I lack greatly; and I cannot endure the thought that my children must lack as greatly, while multitudes are going so far in advance, no better qualified by nature than they. I want you to send me quite a number of names of your leading characters; if it should seem strange to you that I make the demand I will explain it to you when I get there. I want you to answer every item of this letter, and as much more as can have any bearing on my mind either way. Whether you accept this letter kindly or not, I want you to write me an answer without delay. Are there meetings for us to attend? Do you have singing schools? I do thus far feel friendly to your society. Direct my letter to New York —

To the leading members of the Roxbury Community, near Boston.

DEAR SIR, — It gives me the most sincere pleasure to reply to the inquiries proposed in your favor of the 31st instant. I welcome the extended and increasing interest which is manifested in our apparently humble enterprise, as a proof that it is founded in nature and truth, and as a cheering omen of its ultimate success. Like yourself, we are seekers of universal truth. We worship only reality. We are striving to establish a mode of life which shall combine the enchantments of poetry with the facts of daily experience. This we believe can be done by a rigid adherence to justice, by fidelity to human rights, by loving and honoring man as man, by rejecting all arbitrary, factitious distinctions. We are not in the interest of any sect, party, or coterie; we have faith in the soul of man, in the universal soul of things. Trusting to the might of benignant Providence which is over all, we are here sowing in weakness a seed which will be raised in power. But I need not dwell on these general considerations, with which you are doubtless familiar.

In regard to the *connection* of a family with us, our arrangements are liberal and comprehensive. We are not bound by fixed rules which apply to all cases. One general principle we are obliged to adhere to rigidly : not to receive any person who would increase the expenses more than the revenue of the establishment. Within the limits of this principle we can make any arrangement which shall suit particular cases.

A family with resources sufficient for self-support, independent of the exertion of its members, would find a favorable situation with us for the education of its children and for social enjoyment. An annual payment of $1,000 would probably cover the ex penses of board and instruction, supposing that no services were rendered to diminish the expense. An investment of $5,000 would more than meet the original outlay required for a family of eight persons; but in that case an additional appropriation would be needed, either of productive labor or of cash to meet the current expenditures. I forward you herewith a copy of our Prospectus, from which you will perceive that the whole expense of a pupil with us, including board in vacations, is $250 per annum; but in case of one or more pupils remaining with us for a term of years, and assisting in the labors of the establishment, a deduction of one or two dollars per week would be made, according to the services rendered, until such time as, their education being so far completed, they might defray all their expenses by their labor. In the case of your son fifteen years of age, it would be necessary for him to reside with us for three months, at least, on the usual terms; and if, at the end of that time, his services should be found useful, he might continue by paying $150 or $200 per annum, according to the value of his labors; and if he should prove to have a gift for active industry, in process of time he might defray his whole expenses, complete his education, and be fitted for practical life. With the intelligent zeal which you manifest in our enterprise, I need not say that we highly value your sympathy, and should rejoice in any arrangement which might bring us into closer relations. It is only from the faith and love of those whose hearts are filled with the hopes of a better future for humanity that we look for the building up of our "city of God.'

10

So far we have been prospered in our highest expectations. We are more and more convinced of the beauty and justice of our mode of life. We love to breathe this pure, healthy atmosphere; we feel that we are living in the bosom of Nature, and all things seem to expand under the freedom and truth which we worship in our hearts.

I should regret to think that this was to be our last communication with each other. May I not hope to hear from you again? And with the sincere wish that your views of the philosophy of life may bring you still nearer to us, I am, with great respect,

Sincerely your friend,

GEO. RIPLEY.

This will serve to give an idea of Mr. Ripley's personal faith in the enterprise he had undertaken. The letter which follows is of similar purport. With him, as with his comrades, the enthusiasm was genuine and noble, the fruit of highest sentiment and serenest faith, — never gushing or windy, but calm, steady, luminous, and all the more penetrating because reposing on moral principles. Page after page of his note-books is filled with close calculations respecting the capacity of land for tillage: so much corn to the acre, so much grain, so much clover, so much grass, fodder, root, potato, vegetable, — all showing how practical was his enthusiasm.

My dear Sir, — I thank you for sending me the circular calling a convention at Skeneateles for the promotion of the community movement. I have just enjoyed a short visit from Mr. Collins, who explained to me very fully the purposes of the enterprise, and described the advantages of the situation which had been selected as the scene of the initiatory experiment. I hardly need to say that the movers in this noble effort have my warmest sympathy, and that if circumstances permitted I would not deprive myself of the privilege of being present at their deliberations. I am, however, just now so involved in cares and labors that I could not be absent for so long a time without neglect of duty.

Although my present strong convictions are in favor of coöperative association rather than of community of property, I look with an indescribable interest on every attempt to redeem society from its corruptions. The evils arising from trade and money, it appears to me, grow out of the defects of our social organization, not from an intrinsic vice in the things themselves; and the abolition of private property, I fear, would so far destroy the independence of the individual as to interfere with the great object of all social reforms ; namely, the development of humanity, the substitution of a race of free, noble, holy men and women instead of the dwarfish and mutilated specimens which now cover the earth. The great problem is to guarantee individualism against the masses on the one hand, and the masses against the individual on the other.

In society as now organized the many are slaves to
a few favored individuals in a community. I should
dread the bondage of the individual to the power of
the masses ; while association, by identifying the interests of the many and the few, the less gifted and
the highly gifted, secures the sacred personality of
all, gives to each individual the largest liberty of the
children of God. Such are my present views, subject to any modification which farther light may produce. Still I consider the great question of the means
of human regeneration yet open ; indeed hardly
touched as yet, and Heaven forbid that I should not
at least give you my best wishes for the success of
your important enterprise. In our own little Association we practically adopt many community elements. We are eclectics and learners ; but day by
day increases our faith and joy in the principle of
combined industry, and of bearing each other's burdens instead of seeking every man his own. It will
give me great pleasure to hear from you whenever
you may have anything to communicate interesting
to the general movement. I feel that all who are
seeking the emancipation of man are brothers,
though differing in the measures which they may
adopt for that purpose. And from our different
points of view it is not perhaps presumption to hope
that we may aid each other by faithfully reporting
the aspects of earth and sky as they pass before our
field of vision. One danger, of which no doubt you
are aware, proceeds from the growing interest in the
subject ; and that is, the crowd of converts who de-

sire to help themselves rather than to help the movement. It is as true now as it was of old, that he
who would follow this new Messiah must deny himself, and take up his cross daily, or he cannot enter
the promised kingdom. The path of transition is
always covered with thorns, and marked with the
bleeding feet of the faithful. This truth must not
be covered up in describing the paradise for which
we hope. We must drink the water of Marah in the
desert, that others may feed on the grapes of Eshcol.
We must depend on the power of self-sacrifice in man,
not on appeals to his selfish nature, for the success of
our efforts. We should hardly be willing to accept
of men or money unless called for by earnest convictions that they are summoned by a divine voice. I
wish to hear less said to capitalists about a profitable
investment of their funds, as if the holy cause of humanity was to be speeded onward by the same force
which constructs railroads and ships of war. Rather
preach to the rich, " Sell all that you have and give
to the poor, and you shall have treasure in heaven."

To the ordinary members of the Association
the daily life was both stimulating and entertaining. They had amusements in plenty.
There was an Amusement Group, whose business it was to enliven the leisure hours with
charades, tableaux, dances, picnics, theatricals,
.eadings, games, diversions in the woods or in
the house. Hawthorne describes a picnic party
at Brook Farm, in which the grass, vines, trees,

houses, cattle, gypsies, fortune-tellers, negroes, were combined picturesquely with the fanciful dresses of the more elegant spectators. "The household," he remarks, "being composed in great measure of children and young people, is generally a cheerful one enough even in gloomy weather." "It would," he says, "be difficult to conceive beforehand how much can be added to the enjoyment of a household by mere sun‧niness of temper and liveliness of disposition." We may add that sunniness of temper became habitual and permanent, the exasperating causes of friction, so constant in ordinary existence, being removed. The innocent freedom of Brook Farm was stimulating to good-humor, and conducive to happy conditions of mind. A writer in "The Atlantic Monthly" of October, 1878, — a lady of much refinement, a good observer and a frank narrator, — sums up her experience in these words : "Naturally exclusive and fastidious, a spell was woven around me which entered into my very heart, and led me to nobler and higher thoughts than the world ever gave me." Margaret Fuller was at first annoyed by the apparent rudeness of behavior, but was afterwards affected by the simplicity and sincerity she saw everywhere about her. "The first day or two here," she wrote, "is desolate. You seem to belong to nobody. But very soon you learn to take care of yourself, and the freedom of the place is delightful." At one of her conversations she was disturbed by the careless ways of the listeners. " The people showed a good deal of the *sans culotte* tendency in their manner, throwing themselves on the floor, yawning, and going out when they had heard enough. Yet, as the majority differ from me to begin with, — that being the reason the subject (education) was chosen, — they showed, on the whole, more respect and interest than I had expected." A year later she finds " the tone of society much sweeter. . . . There is a pervading spirit of mutual tolerance with great sincerity. There is no longer a passion for grotesque freaks of liberty, but a disposition rather to study and enjoy the liberty of law." Her tribute to the consistent dignity of Mr. and Mrs. Ripley accords with the uniform testimony of all who had knowledge of the institution.

To understand the spirit of Brook Farm, as it was illustrated in its details, one should read the articles in " The Atlantic Monthly " for 1878, and in " Old and New " for February, April, and September, 1871, and May, 1872. Should Dr. J. T. Codman, of Boston, publish his " Recollections," all who are interested in the minute circumstances of the undertaking will have their curiosity abundantly gratified.

The literature of Brook Farm is scattered, but it is not meagre, and it overflows with a spirit of joy. The magazine papers referred to are delightful contributions to the sum of mental entertainment. After making full allowance for the effect of distance in lending enchantment to the view, for the writer's desire to set forth the romantic aspects of a chosen theme, for the poetic sentiment which idealizes the past, and, in general, for an amiable disposition to recall only what was pleasant, there remains enough to make the outsider feel that for a brief period a truly golden age visited the earth. Genius, taste, invention, feeling, put forth their best endeavors; tempers were firm and fine ; excellent gifts were discovered and appreciated ; every kind of talent was exercised ; every species of good nature was encouraged ; every contribution, from the greatest to the least, was heartily welcomed. Spiritual and intellectual, as well as æsthetic, powers were in fairest bloom.

They who would penetrate more deeply into the philosophical idea of the institution may consult Noyes's " History of American Socialisms," or Semler's " Geschichte der Socialismus and Communismus in Nord America," but no formal treatise will convey the genius which inspired and sustained Brook Farm. The editor of the New York "Sun," one of the earliest, ablest, most constant, and most influential friends of the enterprise, said, in a keenly discerning and soberly eulogistic article on Mr. Ripley, then just deceased : " It is not too much to say, that every person who was at Brook Farm for any length of time has ever since looked back upon it with a feeling of satisfaction. The healthy mixture of manual and intellectual labor, the kindly and unaffected social relations, the absence of everything like assumption or servility, the amusements, the discussions, the friendships, the ideal and poetical atmosphere which gave a charm to life, — all these combine to create a picture toward which the mind turns back with pleasure, as to something distant and beautiful, not elsewhere met with amid the routine of this world." Hawthorne, notwithstanding a certain amount of personal disappointment, and a rather passionately expressed opinion against its principle of combining intellectual with manual labor, could speak, in 1852, of " his old and affectionately remembered home at Brook Farm " as being " certainly the most romantic episode in his life." It is unnecessary to repeat here what has been said so often and so authoritatively, that the " Blithedale Romance " simply borrowed from Brook Farm some suggestions of character and a few touches of local color, but was neither intended nor received as an account of the Association. The artist did as painters do, — used the material in his possession, and produced his effects by such combinations as suited his purposes. His work reflects upon Brook Farm neither credit nor discredit. In 1877 a pupil of Brook Farm, living in Boston, made an effort to bring together the old brotherhood for a few hours of social enjoyment. They were widely separated; they had become old; they were worn by toil and care; they were absorbed in life's relations and occupied with life's duties. But they replied in terms of gratitude for the remembrance, of affection towards their former comrades, and of confidence in the principles of their ancient organization. The leader wrote: " Brook Farm may well point to the children who graced her social circles so long time ago, and who have since ripened into strong men and noble women, saying, with the modest pride of the Roman matron, ' These are my jewels.' " Mr. Dana recalled the past affectionately, acknowledging it as a " great pleasure to look back upon the days when we were together, and to believe that the ends for which we then labored are sure at last, in good time, to be realized for mankind." Mr. Channing wrote " The faith and longing for the perfect organization of society have only deepened with time.'

Another said : " Were I not occupied exactly as I am, I should indulge myself, at the cost of a good deal of effort even, in the pleasure of a meeting with fellow-laborers whose faith in the truth of our social principles has never faltered, I am sure, any more than my own." Another wrote : " There is no part of my past life that I recall more frequently than that spent at Brook Farm." Another wished that his " children could live under such influences, that, on the whole, were so pure and refined." Yet another " modest worker " recorded his faith that, " although the original objects of the Association were never accomplished exactly as proposed," he has always felt, in his own case, that he " derived a lasting impulse and gain from the connection."

The daily life at Brook Farm was, of course, extremely simple, even homely. The meals were eaten in the common dining-room, the vegetarians, of whom there were several, occupying a table by themselves. The food was plain. There were no hired waiters. The benches were of pine wood, without backs. There was a general parlor, and a reading-room well sup plied with journals and daily papers. Those who had books readily lent them to such as wished them, or contributed them to the community. Mr. Ripley had his library at the

"Eyrie," as the house was called. There were no separate parlors. The only kitchen was in the " Hive." As the members increased, additional accommodation was provided by the erection of new buildings, but there was at no time too much room for the one hundred and fifty inmates. The forms of courtesy were at all times observed, something better than politeness prompting the associates to make themselves pleasant to their companions. There were naturally few rules, but such as existed were cheerfully obeyed. The highest moral refinement prevailed in all departments. In the morning, every species of industrial activity went on. In the afternoon, the laborers changed their garments and became teachers, often of abstruse branches of knowledge. The evenings were devoted to such recreations as suited the taste of the individual. The farm was never thoroughly tilled, from the want of sufficient hands. A good deal of hay was raised, and milk was produced from a dozen cows. The milk was sold to outside consumers, and the vegetables, so far as they were not wanted in the Association, were sent to the nearest market. Some worked all day in the field, some only a few hours, some none at all, being otherwise employed, or by some reason disqualified. The most cultivated worked the hard

est. Labor-saving machines were introduced or
invented ; but, although all worked who could,
the labor to be done was always in excess of the
laborers.

The serious difficulties were financial. These
pressed heavily on the directors, for no industry, no patience, no devotion will carry on an
enterprise without money. None of the members were rich ; most of them were poor ; the
ablest were only moderately well-to-do. The
trades lacked a market, and therefore did not
thrive. The manufacture of Britannia ware,
lamps and so forth, had limited encouragement ;
the sash and blind maker had leisure in excess
of his orders ; the shoe business languished.
The farm yielded but moderate returns beyond
the actual needs of the community. None of
the lighter industries — nursery, garden, green-
house — paid anything. The necessity of meeting the dues of interest on capital advanced
about exhausted the proceeds of the school,
which was much the most lucrative department
of the institution. The public took no "solid"
interest in the concern. The experienced men
who were there brought little beside their skill.
The subjoined condensed report best tells this
part of the story.

" The direction of finance respectfully submit their
Annual Report for the year ending October 31,
1844 : —

The income of the Association during the year from all sources whatever, has been . . .	$11,854.4
And its expenditures for all purposes, including interest, losses by bad debts, and damage of buildings and tools and furniture . . .	10,409.14
Leaving a balance of	$1,445.27
From which, deducting the amount of doubtful debts contracted this year	284.43
which is to be divided according to the Constitution, we have	$1,160.84

By the last yearly report of this direction it appeared that the Association had been a loser up to November 1, 1843, to the amount of $2,748.83. In this amount were included sundry debts against associates amounting to $924.38, which should not have been included. There were also some small discrepancies, which were afterwards discovered, so that on settling the books the entire deficit appeared to be $1,837. To this amount should be added the proportion of the damage done to the tools, furniture, and general fixtures, and depreciation in the live stock, by the use of the two years which the Association had been in operation previous to that time. The whole damage of this property by the use of these years has been ascertained by inventory to be $365.54, according to the estimates and statements prepared by Messrs. Ryckman and Hastings, which are herewith submitted. Of this sum, $365.54, we have one third, $121.85, to the account of the current year; and two thirds, $243.69, to the account of the two preceding years. To the same account should also be added sundry debts which have since proved to be bad, amounting to $678.08 ; and also an error in favor of ——, amounting to $17.74, which has since been discovered in his account, so that the total deficit of the preceding years will appear to be as follows : —

Deficit on settling the books	$1,837.00
Damage on furniture and fixtures . . .	243.69
Bad debts, including debts of associates, considered doubtful	698.08
J. Morton	17.74
Total,	$2,776.51

From this amount is to be deducted the value of the farm produce, consisting of hay, roots, manures, etc., on hand November 1, 1843, which was not taken into the account of last year; but which has been ascertained to be $762.50, as well as the value $49.13 of the family stores which were on hand at the same time, but were also omitted from the account. Deducting these two amounts, $762.50 and $49.13 ($811.63), from the deficit as above stated, we have : —

Deficit	$2,776.51
Farm produce and family stores	811.63
Real deficit for 1842 and 1843	$1,964.88

It was the opinion of a majority at least of this board that this sum must be chargeable upon the future industry of the Association, and that no dividend could be declared until 't had been made up. Accordingly the quarterly statement for the quarter ending August 1, 1844, was based upon this opinion, and a deficit of $526.78 declared to exist at that time. It is but justice to say that this statement was made up in the absence of one of the members of the direction, who, on seeing it, objected entirely to the principle which it embodied.

The earlier losses of the establishment must be regarded as the price of much valuable experience, and as inevitable in starting such an institution Almost every business fails to pay its expenses at the commencement; it always costs something to set the wheels in operation; this is not, however, to be regarded as absolute loss. This is the view which is to be taken of the condition of the Association at the beginning of the present year: a certain sum had been expended in establishing the Association, but it is not therefore a loss, but only so much capital invested, and well and profitably invested.

To some persons it may perhaps seem remarkable that a dividend should be declared, when the Association is so much in want of ready money as at present; but a little reflection will show any one that it is a perfectly legitimate proceeding. A very large part of our industry has been engaged in the production of permanent property such as the shop, the phalanstery, and the improvements upon the farm. These are of even more value to the Association than so much money, and a dividend may as justly be based upon them as upon cash in the treasury.

In the schedule marked "D" is contained a statement of the debts of the Association contracted since April 17, 1844, by which it appears that those debts amount to $809.96. Of this amount the bills of Messrs. Guild and Hartshorn for blacksmithing, $99.39, are provided for and will presently be settled.

The schedule marked G contains a statement of the time employed by individual associates in labor; and in the schedule marked H is contained a similar account of the time employed in labor by the different probationers.

According to the Constitution, Art. III., Section 4, pupils over ten years of age and probationers are entitled to no fixed dividend, but to such an amount as the Association may decide. In the case of pupils the direction have not thought that any dividend should be awarded. To the probationers the direction would recommend that two thirds of a full dividend should be allowed, which is the proportion that they were thought to be entitled to in fixing the amount of their stipend.

In Schedule C is contained a statement of the amount of interest and insurance which the Association is now paying, which appears to be $1,752.44.

As soon as the phalanstery shall be completed, it will become necessary to establish different rates of room rent. It is a matter of doubt whether such an arrangement is not already desirable. In our present crowded condition indeed the general inconveniences are distributed with tolerable equality; but still it is impossible to avoid some exceptions, and it might contribute to the harmony of the Association

11

if a just graduation of rates for different apartments
should now be established. As far as possible no
member should be the recipient of peculiar favors;
but where all are charged at an equal rate for un-
equal accommodations this is unavoidable. For the
same reason a difference should be made between the
price of board at the Graham tables and those which
are furnished with a different kind of food. It is only
by this means that justice can be done and the constant recurrence of very unpleasant difficulties prevented.

This direction would also call the attention of the
Association to the necessity of instituting suitable
regulations respecting the absence of members. The
right to withdraw from the labors of the Association
is laid down in the Constitution, Art. III., Section 3,
together with the conditions of doing so; but of absence from the Association and its conditions nothing
is said, either in the Constitution or the By-Laws. It
is plain, however, that the absence of any members
from the place for personal purposes ought not to ab-
solve them from the pecuniary responsibilities of the
relation. An equitable share of the current general
expenses should be borne by all members when absent as well as when present. The services of each
member are, by the terms of the compact, supposed
to be of value to the whole phalanx over and above
the guaranties and dividends which he receives as a
compensation. When he withdraws from labor and
yet remains upon the place, this is made up by his
paying the full price for board and other articles fur

nished him; but when he is absent from the place, it is not, according to our present arrangements, made up in any way whatever.

It is also the opinion of the direction that the time has arrived when the natural differences in labor should be recognized and different rates of compensation for attractive, useful, and necessary labor established. In the earlier stages of the enterprise it was, perhaps, not necessary that this should be done, but at present it ought not to be deferred. Indeed, the whole organization of industry should be brought to a greater degree of scientific completeness. It is remarkable that in all young associations much labor seems to be lost; no man appears to accomplish his usual amount of work. This evil can be remedied only by perfecting our groups and series according to scientific principles. The results of the year just passed, not brilliant certainly, but yet highly encouraging, are mainly owing to the imperfect approach to such principles which we have been able to introduce. Even with the present arrangements we presume that the results of next year's settlement might considerably exceed those of the present, but they must still fall far short of what we wish for. Our object will not be gained until we show practically that associated industry gives a product far superior to that of "civilized" industry. The establishment of the three great divisions of labor of which we have spoken, and such other alterations in the general regulations respecting labor as will bring them nearer to justice and to scientific truth, will be important steps to this end.

But we are convinced that it can be fully reached
only by perfectly arranged groups and series, and we
may be sure that the industrial capacities of the Association will increase in compound proportion to the
completeness with which it attains to a regular serial
order in all departments, and to its general harmony.
In conclusion, the direction would respectfully urge
this subject upon the attention of the Association as
one of great and pressing importance.

Charles Anderson Dana, Chairman.

Brook Farm, *December* 15, 1844.

Through all this embarrassment Mr. Ripley
kept his serenity undisturbed. More than that,
he was cheerful and even gay. No cloud was
seen on his face. He had pleasant words for
all. His voice was musical, his manner bright.
Thinking, working with hand, head, heart : ad-
vising, directing, talking philosophy with Theodore Parker, talking farming with Minot Pratt,
writing diplomatic letters, milking cows, carrying vegetables to market, cleaning the stable, —
he was still the same sunny-tempered man, true
to his ideal, and true to himself. His devoted
wife toiled and served at his side unmurmur-
ingly. For ten hours at a time she has been
known to labor in the muslin room. With her
hands in the wash-tub, or her knees on the
scrubbing floor, she would still entertain her
fellow-workers by her smiling wit. Making

courteous apologies to her city friends for not receiving or returning their visits, she never declined repulsive duty or uncongenial companionship. A diligent and laborious housekeeper, she was yet so attentive to her classes that in two years she missed only two recitations ; and with all this, she was so unassuming that her name scarcely appears on the record of Brook Farm. She was an adviser, too, — one of the Council, — as intimately connected with the administration of the community as with its toils. Much of the energy of Mr. and Mrs. Ripley must have been due to sheer character. None had so much to lose as they. Upon none did the burden of care rest so heavily. They had less share than the rest in the amusements and recreations of the place. They were no longer young. They had already a background of disappointment. In thoughtful hours their future must have seemed precarious. But nothing of this appeared. From morning till night they upheld the courage and faith of those younger and less anxious than themselves. This they did, every day, for six or seven years, waiting and hoping, refusing to be discouraged, concealing from others, as far as possible hiding from themselves, the suspicion that the prayer, " Thy will be done on earth as it is in heaven," was not so near being answered as they had believed.

CHAPTER IV.

BROOK FARM. — FOURIERISM.

THUS far there had been no organization. In fact, disorganization had been the rule of the institution. The name was an after-thought. The Constitution was not written till the experiment was several months old. The principle of freedom from all restraints but those of reason and conscience made the managers jealous even of apparent control. The policy of non-intervention was carried as far as it could be without incurring the risk of anarchy. This was not unfitly called the "transcendental" period. It was charming, but unprofitable in a worldly sense. As early as 1843 the wisdom of making changes in the direction of scientific arrangement was agitated; in the first months of 1844 the reformation was seriously begun. On January 15, 1844, W. H. Channing, editor of the "Present," a weekly paper begun in September, 1843, published in New York, wrote a glowing account of a convention which had been held at Boston on the last week of December, 1843, and the first week of January, 1844,

in behalf of Fourierism. In the closing number of the "Dial," April, 1844, Miss E. P.
Peabody called attention to the same meeting.
The attendance was considerable, and the interest so great that the convention, which was
to have broken up on Wednesday, held over
through Thursday and Friday. At this convention Brook Farm was represented, and Mr.
Ripley made an earnest speech. The "Phalanx "— an organ of Fourier's doctrine, also
published in New York since October, 1843 —
welcomed Brook Farm to the scientific fraternity in an article printed February 5, 1844. In
connection with the proposed transformation,
the directors of the Brook Farm Association
published a second edition of their Constitution, with the following " Introductory Statement." We print the statement, which shows
how early the change to Fourierism was virtually made. That so complete a revolution was
effected without long and eager discussion, some
misgiving, much criticism, and a good deal of
discontent, especially among the irresponsible
members, is not to be supposed. The idyllic
phase of Brook Farm was well-nigh ended.

INTRODUCTORY STATEMENT.

The Association at Brook Farm has now been in
existence upwards of two years. Originating in the

thought and experience of a few individuals, it has hitherto worn for the most part the character of a private experiment, and has avoided rather than sought the notice of the public. It has, until the present time, seemed fittest to those engaged in this enterprise to publish no statements of their purposes or methods, to make no promises or declarations, but quietly and sincerely to realize, as far as might be possible, the great ideas which gave the central impulse to their movement. It has been thought that a steady endeavor to embody these ideas more and more perfectly in life would give the best answer, both to the hopes of the friendly and the cavils of the skeptical, and furnish in its results the surest grounds for any larger efforts.

Meanwhile, every step has strengthened the faith with which we set out; our belief in a divine order of human society has in our own minds become an absolute certainty; and considering the present state of humanity and of social science, we do not hesitate to affirm that the world is much nearer the attainment of such a condition than is generally supposed.

The deep interest in the doctrine of Association, which now fills the minds of intelligent persons everywhere, indicates plainly that the time has passed when even initiative movements ought to be prosecuted in silence, and makes it imperative on all who have either a theoretical or practical knowledge of the subject to give their share to the stock of public information.

Accordingly we have taken occasion, at several

public meetings recently held in Boston, to state some of the results of our studies and experience, and we desire here to say emphatically, that while, on the one hand, we yield an unqualified assent to that doctrine of universal unity which Fourier teaches, so, on the other, our whole observation has shown us the truth of the practical arrangements which he deduces therefrom. The law of groups and series is, we are convinced, the law of human nature, and when men are in true social relations, their industrial organization will necessarily assume those forms.

But beside the demand for information respecting the principles of Association, there is a deeper call for action in the matter. We wish, therefore, to bring Brook Farm before the public, as a location offering at least as great advantages for a thorough experiment as can be found in the vicinity of Boston. It is situated in West Roxbury, three miles from the depot of the Dedham Branch Railroad, and about eight miles from Boston, and combines a convenient nearness to the city with a degree of retirement and freedom from unfavorable influences, unusual even in the country. The place is one of great natural beauty, and, indeed, the whole landscape is so rich and various as to attract the notice even of casual visitors. The farm now owned by the Association contains two hundred and eight acres, of as good quality as any land in the neighborhood of Boston, and can be enlarged by the purchase of land adjoining to any necessary extent. The property now in the hands of the Association is worth nearly or quite thirty thousand dollars, of which about twenty two thousand dollars is invested either in the stock of the company, or in permanent loans to it at six per cent., which can remain as long as the Association may wish.

The fact that so large an amount of capital is already invested and at our service as the basis of more extensive operations, furnishes a reason why Brook Farm should be chosen as the scene of that practical trial of Association which the public feeling calls for in this immediate vicinity, instead of forming an entirely new organization for that purpose.

The completeness of our educational department is also not to be overlooked. This has hitherto received our greatest care, and in forming it we have been particularly successful. In any new Association it must be many years before so many accomplished and skillful teachers in the various branches of intellectual culture could be enlisted. Another strong reason is to be found in the degree of order our organization has already attained, by the help of which a large Association might be formed without the losses and inconveniences which would otherwise necessarily occur. The experience of nearly three years in all the misfortunes and mistakes incident to an undertaking so new and so little understood, carried on throughout by persons not entirely fitted for the duties they have been compelled to perform, has, as we think, prepared us to assist in the safe-conduct of an extensive and complete Association.

Such an institution, as will be plain to all, cannot

by any sure means, be brought at once and full grown into existence. It must, at least in the present state of society, begin with a comparatively small number of select and devoted persons, and increase by natural and gradual aggregations. With a view to an ultimate expansion into a perfect Phalanx, we desire without any delay to organize the three primary departments of labor, namely, Agriculture, Domestic Industry, and the Mechanic Arts.

For this purpose, additional capital will be needed, which it is most desirable should be invested by those who propose to connect themselves personally with the institution. These should be men and women accustomed to labor, skillful, careful, in good health, and, more than all, imbued with the idea of Association, and ready to consecrate themselves without reserve to its realization. For it ought to be known that the work we propose is a difficult one, and, except to the most entire faith and resolution, will offer insurmountable obstacles and discouragements. Neither will it be possible to find in Association, at the outset, the great outward advantages it ultimately promises. The first few years must be passed in constant and unwearied labor, lightened chiefly by the consciousness of high aims and the inward content that devotion to a universal object cannot fail to bring. Still there are certain tangible compensations which Association guarantees immediately. These are freedom from pecuniary anxiety and the evils of competitive industry, free and friendly society, and the education of children. How great these are, those who have felt the terrible burdens which the present civilized society imposes in these respects will not need to be informed.

Those who may wish to further this cause by investments of money only, will readily perceive that their end is not likely to be lost in an Association whose means are devoted mainly to productive industry, and where nothing will ever be risked in uncertain speculations.

The following Constitution is the same as that under which we have hitherto acted, with such alterations as, on a careful revision, seemed needful. All persons who are not familiar with the purposes of Association will understand from this document that we propose a radical and universal reform, rather than to redress any particular wrong, or to remove the sufferings of any single class of human beings. We do this in the light of universal principles, in which all differences, whether of religion, or politics, or philosophy, are reconciled, and the dearest and most private hope of every man has the promise of fulfillment. Herein, let it be understood, we would remove nothing that is truly beautiful or venerable; we reverence the religious sentiment in all its forms, the family, and whatever else has its foundation either in human nature or the Divine Providence. The work we are engaged in is not destruction, but true conservation; it is not a mere revolution, but, as we are assured, a necessary step in the course of social progress which no one can be blind enough to think has yet reached its limit. We believe that humanity trained by these long centuries of suffering and struggle, led onward by so many saints and heroes and sages, is at length prepared to enter into that universal order towards which it has perpetually moved. Thus we recognize the worth of the whole Past, and of every doctrine and institution it has bequeathed us ; thus, also, we perceive that the Present has its own high mission, and we shall only say what is beginning to be seen by all sincere thinkers, when we declare that the imperative duty of this time and this country, — nay more, that its only salvation, and the salvation of all civilized countries, — lies in the reorganization of society, according to the unchanging laws of human nature and of universal harmony.

We look, then, to the generous and hopeful of all classes for sympathy, for encouragement, and for actual aid, not to ourselves only, but to all those who are engaged in this great work. And, whatever may be the result of any special efforts, we can never doubt that the object we have in view will finally be attained ; that human life shall yet be developed, not in discord and misery, but in harmony and joy, and the perfected earth shall at last bear on her bosom a race of men worthy of the name.

GEORGE RIPLEY,   }
MINOT PRATT,   } *Directors.*
CHARLES A. DANA, }

BROOK FARM, WEST ROXBURY,
    January 18, 1844.

The most prominent person associated with the name and doctrines of Fourier in this country, and the most powerful instrument in the conversion of Brook Farm, was Mr. Albert Brisbane. He had studied the system in France, and made it his business to introduce it here. His book, "The Social Destiny of Man," was published in 1840; in 1843 the New York "Tribune" opened its columns to him; in the autumn of the same year the monthly "Phalanx" was started. Mr. Brisbane was interested in the Brook Farm experiment, and naturally desirous of giving it a more scientific basis. He came there often, at first spending a few days, but finally residing there several months. He took no part in the manual labor of the place, but devoted himself to the translation of Fourier's Works and to the exposition of his theory. He was a man of ability and enthusiasm, an intellectual visionary. To his fancy the heavens were opened to Fourier, and the kingdom of God was ready to descend from the clouds upon his disciples. In the mere name 'Phalanx," he seemed to hear the trumpets of the angels. It is probable that from him came the earliest knowledge of Fourier's system, as well as the impulse to convert to it the leaders of the movement in West Roxbury. On the 4th of April, 1844, a convention of Associationists was held in Clinton Hall, New York. George Ripley presided; among the Vice-Presidents were Horace Greeley, Albert Brisbane, and Charles A. Dana; the business committee comprised, besides those already named, Parke Godwin and William H. Channing. The spirit of Fourier ruled the convention, though exception was taken to such of his doctrines as, in the opinion of the more sober-minded or scrupulous, were inconsistent with the precepts of the New Testament, or the established customs of society in New England. The speeches were eloquent, the letters were glowing, the resolutions were brave. Burning words fell as from inspired lips. Channing, Dana, Greeley, Godwin — each in characteristic style and all with deep sincerity — poured out their souls; Mr. Solyman Brown of the Leroysville Phalanx, recited an ode, entitled " Visions of the Future." The convention was closed with prayer and benediction.

The change to Fourierism introduced essential modifications into the Constitution of Brook Farm; a different class of people, more practical and prosaic, came thither. It may be questioned whether the revolution had the sympathy of Mrs. Ripley; but Mr. Ripley threw himself into it with all his ardor, doing his utmost to make it successful. He wrote, talked, lectured, illustrating by word and example the new gospel of labor and love, which to him was another edition of the Gospel of Christ. In March,

1845, the " Brook Farm Phalanx " was incorporated by the Legislature of Massachusetts. The Constitution breathes a spirit of hope which is pathetic at this distance of time, as we look back on the failure of every similar undertaking, and see how helplessly astray was every one of these attempts to reconstruct the social order ; but they reveal a loftiness of sentiment and a vigor of thought which would do honor, under any circumstances, to human nature. The " common sense " of the world has sufficiently vindicated itself in their destruction ; let Faith and Aspiration rejoice in their inauguration and purpose. The sternness of the waking does not destroy the beauty of the dream.

The publication of the Constitution was followed in the summer by " The Harbinger," which became the leading journal of Fourierism in the country. The first number appeared on June 14th. It was a handsome sheet of sixteen pages, printed in quarto form. Its list of contributors was about the most remarkable ever presented. Besides Ripley, Dwight, Dana, and Rykman, of Brook Farm, there were Brisbane, Channing, Curtis, Cranch, Godwin, Greeley, Lowell, Whittier, Story, Higginson, to say nothing of gentlemen less known in literature, journalism, art, and business. The number of Mr. Ripley's papers, longer and shorter, is **over** three hundred. He and Mr. Dana wrote most of the editorial articles, in the interest of Association · Mr. Dana noticed the new books, was the chief reviewer; John S. Dwight had charge of the musical and poetical department, but did not confine himself to it, his zeal prompting him to publish papers advocating Association in general and Fourier's doctrines in particular; G. W. Curtis was a regular New York correspondent, reporting mainly the news in the musical world; W. H. Channing and Parke Godwin translated or selected from Fourier's writings; Whittier sent a poem, "To my Friend on the Death of his Sister;" Lowell, Cranch, Higginson, and Story appear as poets, as do also Dwight and Dana. So many brilliant men excited interest in the paper, and would have insured its success, if brilliancy alone would do it; but even genius, though united with enthusiasm, will not propel a ship in a dead calm, or sustain a kite in a lifeless air. Here is the prospectus: —

"THE HARBINGER:"

Devoted to Social and Political Progress: Published simultaneously at New York and Boston, by the Brook Farm Phalanx.

"All things, at the present day, stand provided and prepared, and await the light."

Under this title it is proposed to publish a weekly newspaper for the examination and discussion of the great questions in social science, politics, literature, and the arts, which command the attention of all believers in the progress and elevation of humanity.

In politics "The Harbinger" will be democratic in its principles and tendencies; cherishing the deepest interest in the advancement and happiness of the masses; warring against all exclusive privilege in legislation, political arrangements, and social customs; and striving, with the zeal of earnest conviction, to promote the triumph of the high democratic faith which it is the chief mission of the nineteenth century to realize in society. Our devotion to the democratic principle will lead us to take the ground of fearless and absolute independence in regard to all political parties, whether professing attachment to that principle or hostility to it. We know that fidelity to an idea can never be measured by adherence to a name; and hence we shall criticise all parties with equal severity, though we trust that the sternness of truth will always be blended with the temperance of impartial candor. With tolerance for all opinions, we have no patience with hypocrisy and pretense; least of all with that specious fraud which would make a glorious principle the apology for personal ends. It will therefore be a leading object of "The Harbinger" to strip the disguise from the prevailing parties, to show them in their true light, to give them due honor, to tender them our grateful reverence whenever we see them true to a noble

principle ; but at all times, and on every occasion, to
expose false professions, to hold up hollow-hearted-
ness and duplicity to just indignation, to warn the
people against the demagogue who would cajole them
by honeyed flatteries, no less than against the devotee
of Mammon who would make them his slaves.

"The Harbinger" will be devoted to the cause of
a radical, organic, social reform, essential to the high
est development of man's nature, to the production
of these elevated and beautiful forms of character of
which he is capable, and to the diffusion of happiness, excellence, and universal harmony upon the
earth. The principles of universal unity as taught
by Charles Fourier, in their application to society,
we believe are at the foundation of all genuine social
progress ; and it will ever be our aim to discuss and
defend these principles without any sectarian bigotry,
and in the catholic and comprehensive spirit of their
great discoverer. While we bow to no man as an
authoritative, infallible master, we revere the genius
of Fourier too highly not to accept with joyful welcome the light which he has shed on the most intricate problems of human destiny.

The social reform, of whose advent the signs are
everywhere visible, comprehends all others ; and in
laboring for its speedy accomplishment, we are conscious of devotion to the enslaved, to the promotion
of genuine temperance, and to the elevation of the
toiling and down-trodden masses to the inborn rights
of humanity.

In literature "The Harbinger" will exercise a firm

and impartial criticism without respect of persons or parties. It will be made a vehicle for the freest thought, though not of random speculations; and with a generous appreciation of the various forms of truth and beauty, it will not fail to expose such instances of false sentiment, perverted taste and erroneous opinion, as may tend to vitiate the public mind or degrade the individual character. Nor will the literary department of "The Harbinger" be limited to criticism alone. It will receive contributions from various pens in different spheres of thought; and, free from dogmatic exclusiveness, will accept all that in any way indicates the unity of man with Man, with Nature, and with God. Consequently, all true science, all poetry and art, all sincere literature, all religion that is from the soul, all wise analyses of mind and character, will come within its province.

We appeal for aid in our enterprise to the earnest and hopeful spirits in all classes of society. We appeal to all who, suffering from a restless discontent in the present order of things, with faith in man and trust in God, are striving for the establishment of universal justice, harmony, and love. We appeal to the thoughtful, the aspiring, the generous everywhere, who wish to see the reign of heavenly truth triumphant by supplanting the infernal discords and falsehoods on which modern society is built, for their sympathy, friendship, and practical coöperation in he undertaking which we announce to-day.

The energy with which Mr. Ripley threw himself into the work of establishing a Phalanx

at Brook Farm, on Fourier's system, may be in-
ferred from the following letter of Mr. Brisbane,
which belongs to this period. The translations
spoken of were made from the writings of Fourier, and may be found in the second volume of
the "Sociological Series," published in New
York by C. P. Somerby, 1876. A lecture on
Fourier, mostly biographical, delivered at this
time, exists in manuscript; it is remarkable
chiefly for its charming clearness of style, and
the firm conviction of its tone, but makes no attempt at exposition.

NEW YORK, *December* 9, 1845.

MY DEAR RIPLEY, — Yours of the 3d, post-marked
the 5th, came to hand yesterday. I note all its contents in relation to your views upon the necessity of
developing Brook Farm. The reason why I have
spoken in some of my last letters of the best means
of bringing B. F. to a close, and making preparations
for a trial under more favorable circumstances, is
this: In the middle of November I received a letter
from Charles Dana, in which, in speaking of the va-
rioloid, he stated the difficulties you have to contend
with, and expressed fears for the future in such a
way, that I concluded you had made up your minds
to bring things to a close. I feared that Morton
might be foreclosing his mortgage, which would be
a most serious affair. This was the cause of my ad-
verting to a possible dissolution, and the necessity of
ooking ahead to meet in the best and most proper
manner such a contingency.

As to my opinion of what is to be done, it is easily explained. 1st. We must raise a sufficient amount of capital, — and the amount must not be small. 2d. When that is secured, we must prepare and work out a plan of scientific organization, sufficiently complete in its details to serve as a guide in organizing an Association. For my own part, I feel no capability whatever of directing an Association by discipline, by ideas of duty, moral suasion, and other similar means. I want organization; I want a mechanism suited and adapted to human nature, so that human nature can follow its laws and affections, and go rightly, and be its own guide. I might do something in directing such an organization, but would be useless in any other way. As we all like to be active, I should like exceedingly to take part in and help construct a scientific organization. How can we raise the capital necessary to do something effectual? I see but two ways. The first, is for Channing and me — and if he will not do it then for you and me — if you could possibly engage in it, to lecture patiently and perseveringly in various parts of the country — having the translation of Fourier with us — and *continue at this work* until we have enlisted and interested men enough who will subscribe each a certain sum sufficient to form the fund we deem necessary. Patience and perseverance would do this. One hundred men who would subscribe $1,000 each would give us a fine capital. Something effectual, I think, might be done with such an amount; less than that I fear would be patch-work. Second. If Channing or you cannot engage in this enterprise, then I shall see what I can do alone. I shall make first the trial of the steel business ; things will now soon be determined, probably in a few weeks ; there are chances that it may be a great thing. If that turns out nothing, then I shall take Fourier's work and do something of what I propose you, or Channing, and I hould do together. If nothing can be done in this way, then I shall wait patiently until I can get my father to embark with his fortune, or come into the control of it — I do not mean the capital, but the income, which will be large, ere long. Such are my prospects. If the capital can be had, where shall we organize, you will ask ? That is a thing to be carefully considered, and which we cannot decide at present. Placed under the circumstances you are, all these speculations will appear foreign to the subject that interests you, and useless.

You want capital, and immediately, for B. F. Now it seems to me a problem as perplexing to get $15,000 for B. F., as it does to raise $100,000. Where can it be had ? The New Yorkers, who have money, are all interested and pledged to raise $10,000 for the N. A. P., to pay off its mortgage. You might as well undertake to raise dead men, as to obtain any considerable amount of capital from the people here. I have tried it so often that I know the difficulties. The fact is, we have a great work to accomplish — that of organizing an Association, and to do it we must have the means adequate to the task, and to get these means we must make the most persevering and

Herculean efforts. We must go at the thing in ear
nest, and labor until we have secured the means. I
really see no other way or avenue to success; if you
do, I should be glad to hear your explanations of it.
Fifteen thousand dollars might do a good deal at B
F., but would it do the thing effectually, that is, make
a trial that would impress the public? — and for
anything short of that, none of us, I suppose, would
labor.

We are surrounded by great difficulties. I see no
immediate chance of obtaining a capital sufficient for
a good experiment, and until we have the capital to
organize upon quite a complete scale, I should say
that it would be a very great misfortune to dissolve
B. F. No uncertain prospects should exercise any
influence; the means must be had in hand before we
make any decisive movement towards a removal, or
organizing in a more favorable location — even if you
were perfectly willing to leave New England and the
neighborhood of Boston. As I said, I spoke of it
and should be urged to make at once the greatest
efforts to obtain capital, only under the fear that circumstances might force a crisis upon you.

I have touched merely upon generalities to-day;
after further correspondence, I will write you more in
detail. I will also come on and see you, if you deem
it advisable. The steel experiment keeps me here at
present. I think that next week I shall test it. I am
getting a furnace built expressly. I am deeply rejoiced to hear that you are getting on so well with the
translation, and expect also to hear you say, that you

wonder that we have done without it so long. It must be the means of converting the minds of those we most want, and which we have not yet been able to reach. Push it ahead as far as possible. I have perfect confidence that you can translate it better than any one else in the world, and it has been left for you to do.

I will forward what can be collected the first moment that it can be obtained. I have not received a second letter from Dwight; if he has written, it has not yet come to hand. Come on with him by all means, if you can, or without him, if he cannot come, or I cannot make my arrangements here for the enterprise which will call him to New York.

Please present my kindest and most respectful regards to Mrs. Ripley, and believe me as ever,

Your true friend,

A. BRISBANE.

"The Harbinger" lived nearly four years, a little more than two at Brook Farm, less than two in New York. The last number was issued on the 10th of February, 1849. It was a weekly sheet, mainly written by Brook Farm men, and to the last edited by Mr. Ripley, whose articles, to say nothing in disparagement of the rest, showed a warmth of heart, an earnestness of soul, a clearness of mind and a force of statement which proved the man's utter sincerity in the cause.

The published writings of this period illustrate the fine enthusiasm which animated the man, but they do not exhibit the affection that he felt for the least of those who shared in any degree his zeal for humanity. The letter which is now printed, written in answer to a friendly missive from a Brook Farm pupil, now a married woman in a western city, supplies this deficiency. It was found among the few papers that he preserved of that happy time : —

March 9, 1880.

MY DEAR ——, — I can never think of you under any other name than that which so deeply interested me in your childhood, in spite of what you tell me of your " dear, kind husband," and your four blooming sons and daughters. It is not too much to say that your charming letter gave me a thrill of pleasure, recalling so vividly the by-gone days, when a child in mind and appearance but a woman in thought and feeling, your original and racy character awakened in me an interest, " a real affection," as you justly called it, which has never for one moment been dimmed from that time to the present. I rejoice more than I can tell you in the kindly and beautiful remembrances which I am constantly receiving from my old pupils and associates of the Brook Farm life, which was then only a name for an enthusiastic endeavor for a purer and better social state, but which has since become celebrated in romance and history Among my own most precious recollections are those of your beloved and honored family, of whom Flor ence is the only one with whom I have kept a personal intercourse, and which has always been in the highest degree pleasant and satisfactory. You do not know that soon after your visit to Mrs. Manning, now more than twenty years ago, my wife was attacked with a fatal disease, and died in the early part of 1861. About five years after I was married to a German lady, several years younger than myself, of admirable character and great personal attractions, who has given a charm to my life for the past fourteen years. I have nearly reached the limit of four-score years, but I find that age thus far makes little difference in my attachment to early friends, in my enjoyment of life, or in my intellectual activity. I beg you to present my cordial greetings to your husband, who will possess the esteem which I cherish for yourself, and my sincere love (for your sake) to the dear children, who have honored me with their kind request. I regret that I have no photograph, as I have been unwilling to sit for one for many years as they are all such fearful caricatures, and at present especially I could only offer the "ashes of roses," which would be an unworthy gift to one who remembers the flower in the fullness of its maturity.

It is unnecessary to speculate on the causes of the failure at Brook Farm. There was every reason why it should fail; there was no earthly, however much heavenly, reason there may have been, why it should succeed. Like similar enterprises elsewhere it was untimely, and whatever is untimely is already doomed to perish. The principle is established that human progress is gradual, by slow stages, evil by degrees yielding to good, the spiritual succeeding the natural by almost imperceptible processes of amelioration; so that all attempts miscarry which aim at results, but disregard the steps by which results are reached. Mankind are repelled, as by an instinct, from undertakings that are not founded on the visible sequence of cause and effect. Capital avoids them. Practical ability shuns them. Neither ambition nor thrift will take part in them. The world, no doubt, is selfish; but so long as it is providentially so, so long as selfishness is one of the stubborn conditions of advance in righteousness, to complain of it is idle, however strenuously one may resist it.

To those who think that Brook Farm failed through lack of organization, it may be replied that it failed quite as probably through having too much. The introduction of Fourierism, from which so much was expected, proved in the end unfortunate. It frightened away idealists whose presence had given to the spot its chief attraction, and injured the pastoral bloom which beautified it. The reputation of Brook Farm for brilliancy, wit, harmless eccentricity, was seriously compromised. The joyous spirit of youth was sobered. The outside community henceforth regarded the enterprise as a mechanical attempt to reform society rather than as a poetic attempt to regenerate it. Fourierism brought in a new set of theorists, quite as unpractical, and much less sunny.

The fire, which destroyed the only "phalanstery," on the evening of March 3, 1846, was a severe blow, — more severe than the people admitted. The edifice was commenced in the summer of 1844, and was in progress until November, 1845, when work was suspended for the winter. It was resumed on the very day of the fire, which was caused by a defect in the construction of a chimney. The structure was of wood, one hundred and seventy-five feet long, three stories high, with spacious attics, divided into pleasant and convenient rooms for single persons. The second and third stories were broken up into fourteen "apartments," independent of each other, each comprising a parlor and three sleeping rooms, connected by piazzas which ran the whole length of the building on both stories. The basement contained a large kitchen, a dining-hall capable of seating from three to four hundred persons, two public saloons, together with a spacious hall and lecture-room. Although by no means a complete model for a phalanstery, it was well adapted to imme-

diate purposes, delightfully situated, and pleas-
ing to the eye.   About $7,000 in all, including
the labor of the associates, had been expended
on the building; it was estimated that $3,000
more would render it fit for its uses.   There
was no insurance on it.   The loss, which was
total, fell upon the holders of partnership stock
and the members of the Association.   Notwithstanding the gallant spirit in which the calamity was met, the loss was serious.   There was
a disposition on the part of the more sanguine
to make light of the disaster; the earnest souls
fell back on their heroism and vowed to perse-
vere in spite of all discouragements.   The noble
president thanked the firemen, who had come
from neighboring towns, cheered the heart of
the desponding, and even drew consolation from
the thought that the building had not become
endeared to them by association; — but it was
in vain.   The blow was staggering.   Councils
of deliberation were held.   Discussion was long
and heated.   Proposals to dissolve were voted
down by men who in their hearts felt that
dissolution was inevitable.   The boldest hoped
against hope.   It may be true that the confla-
gration was not the immediate cause of the ensuing disorganization; but that it was a proxi-
mate cause of it can hardly be doubted.   Cer
tain it is that from that moment the thoughts

of many turned away from Brook Farm. It was harder than ever to obtain capital. There was no demand for stock. It is more than likely that Mr. Greeley's interest was diverted towards projects nearer New York, which looked more promising, which at any rate were more convenient, and which seemed to have before them a future. On Brook Farm itself few attacks, either public or private, were made. Its purpose was so sincere, its conduct so irreproachable, its devotion to ends purely humane so evident, that malice could find no grounds for assailing it. The evil eyes that were turned on it at last were perhaps sharpened by political animosity towards Mr. Greeley, whose unpopularity it was compelled to share. The lash of partisan spite, it was found, could be made to reach him if aimed over the shoulders of a scheme which lent itself so readily to ridicule.

It is not worth while to do more than mention certain disadvantages of Brook Farm which might in any case have impeded its success, but which, under the circumstances, cannot be held in any considerable measure accountable for its failure. The soil was not, on the whole, favorable to profitable tillage; it needed manuring, which was costly, because hard to get. There was no water-power available. Railroad communication with the city was infrequent; so that the heavy work of transportation had to be done by wagon. Local industries in the neighborhood were inadequate to stimulate a demand for various labor. Such obstacles might have been overcome by capital or by trained skill, but both of these would have been needed, and neither of them was supplied. The consequence was a result that was rather æsthetic than mercenary, a harvest that could be " gathered in a song." The idealists lingered last, loath to leave a spot endeared by so many associations, hallowed by so many hopes. One of the last to go, one of the saddest of heart, one of the most self-sacrificing through it all, was John S. Dwight. It may be truly said that Brook Farm died in music.

To Mr. Ripley the disappointment must have been bitter. How bitter is evident from the fact that he never referred to Brook Farm except in intimate conversation with his old comrades, or with one to whom he could unbosom his soul. At times he spoke of it in terms of banter such as one may use to conceal deep feeling ; at other times, though this was rare, he dwelt with solemnity on the aims which sent him thither and kept him there doing the work he did for so many years. His faith in the principles involved remained with him through his life. About a year before his death he ex pressed an earnest conviction of the truth of the primary ideas laid down by Fourier, and a belief that some of his predictions were coming true. Later still he declared his persuasion that the highest visions he had ever entertained must be fulfilled in due time. His weak experiment had come to nothing, but the truth it sought to serve survived. He cast no blame upon the constitution of the world, none upon his fellow-men. His own mistake he might be sorry for, but of the undertaking he could not feel ashamed. Of one thing he could be certain: of his own singleness of purpose, of his own integrity of will. His studies in the philosophy of history had been profound; he had read much and thought much, though he had written little. As a man of letters his activity had been hardly perceptible, but as a man of mind it was of permanent value, and his subsequent service as a man of letters was greatly indebted to the experience acquired at Brook Farm.

The crushing difficulties were, as will have been comprehended long ere this, financial; these pressed more and more heavily, month by month, and at length could not be breasted. The catastrophe came from this quarter, and in such manner as the accompanying documents explain.

BROOK FARM, *March* 4, 1847.

Minutes of a meeting held this day pursuant to a call in writing, through the post-office to each of the stockholders and creditors of the Brook Farm Phalanx. The following persons being present, namely, G. Ripley, J. M. Palisse, Jno. Hoxie, Francis G. Shaw, Geo. R. Russell, S. Butterfield, N. Colton, P. N. Kleinstrup. G. Ripley in the chair. J. M. Palisse was chosen Secretary.

After a verbal statement from G. Ripley respecting the present condition of the Phalanx, it was voted unanimously, that Geo. Ripley be authorized to let the Farm for one year from March 1st, for $350; and the Keith lot for $100 or more, with such conditions and reservations as he may deem best for the interest of the stockholders.

Adjourned.

J. M. PALISSE, *Secretary.*

BROOK FARM, *August* 18, 1847.

Minutes of a meeting of the stockholders and creditors of the Brook Farm Phalanx, held pursuant to due notice given to all parties by George Ripley. Present: Geo. Ripley, Theodore Parker, Samuel Teal, P. N. Kleinstrup, A. Kay, J. M. Palisse, Amelia Russell, Mary Ann Ripley.

J. M. Palisse was appointed Secretary of the meeting. Theodore Parker read a letter from G. R. Russell, authorizing the former to represent him and vote at this meeting. It was then voted unanimously: that the President of the Phalanx be, and is hereby authorized, to transfer to a Board of Three Trustees the whole property of the Corporation for the purpose and with power of disposing of it to the best advantage of all concerned.

Voted unanimously, that Messrs. T. Parker, G. R. Russell, and Samuel P. Teal compose that Board of Trustees.

Voted unanimously, that said Board of Trustees has power to add Mr. Francis Jackson or some suitable person to its number, or employ him as its agent in the management of the business confided to its care.

Adjourned.

J. M. PALISSE, *Secretary.*

The devoted wife, who had toiled unflinchingly by her husband's side, lending the wings of her ardent feeling to the steady momentum of his resolute will, was betraying signs of physical and mental exhaustion. In 1846, the treasured books were sold at auction, carrying with them a purpose never again to collect a library, since never again could books mean to him what those had meant. On the transference of "The Harbinger" to New York in 1847, the home was removed from West Roxbury to the village of Flatbush, on Long Island. There Mrs. Ripley earned money by teaching, while he pursued his editorial labors in a bare, upper room of the old Tribune building. Discomfort in every form was his portion. His chief recreation was a frequent visit to Coney Island, then less gay and less respectable than it is now, and a plunge in the lonely surf. His daily companion was toil. His consolation was the fidelity of a few friends and the loyal affection of his wife. His support was the never-failing determination to do his duty and the uplifting strength of an aspiration which was never clouded for more than a moment. A friend who knew him well during this time speaks with feeling of the cheerful courage with which he bore his fortune, and the sweetness with which he met the onset of calamity. Without jar or fret, jocund in circumstances that would have broken ordinary men, he moved through the laborious weeks, in his home a daily sunshine, in his office a perpetual serenity which concealed a secret sadness so effectually that only the most intimate could suspect its existence. In later life he told with humor to the writer of these lines how, after an attack of illness which took him away from his office for some weeks, he returned to find the room deserted. "The Harbinger" had ended a promising but precarious existence, and he was without place or employment in the world.

The following verses, which belong to this period, — the only lines, so far as is known, that he ever wrote, — tell of his frame of mind.

They are copied from "The Christian Examiner" for May, 1847 : —

"THE ANGELS OF THE PAST."

My buried days! — in bitter tears
  I sit beside your tomb,
And ghostly forms of vanished years
  Flit through my spirit's gloom.

In throngs around my soul they press,
  They fill my dreamy sight
With visions of past loveliness
  And shapes of lost delight.

Like angels of the Lord they move
  Each on his mystic way, —
These blessed messengers of love,
  These heralds of the day.

And as they pass, the conscious air
  Is stirred to music round,
And a murmur of harmonious prayer
  Is breathed along the ground.

And sorrow dies from out my heart
  In exhalations sweet,
And the bands of life, which she did part,
  In blessed union meet.

The past and future o'er my head
  Their sacred grasp entwine,

And the eyes of all the holy dead
　　Around, before me, shine.

And I rise to life and duty,
　　From nights of fear and death,
With a deeper sense of beauty
　　And fuller strength of faith.

CHAPTER V

LABOR.

On the breaking up of Brook Farm, and the decease of "The Harbinger," Mr. Ripley was thrown altogether on his literary resources. In every other direction his outlook was dark. He had made two ventures, neither of which had met his anticipations. He had reached the period of life when the thoughts turn backward. He was poorer than poor, for he was in debt. His noble wife had lost her faith in the ideas that had sustained them both in much hardship, and from the point of another creed, the Roman Catholic, regarded the associative experiment as unfortunate. What remained to him was himself, his mind, his training, his power with the pen, his determination to achieve in other fields what he had failed as yet to accomplish.

His first energies were directed to the task of working himself clear of the pecuniary responsibility for Brook Farm. How great this was cannot now be accurately determined. For a man of ample means it would have been tri-

fling, but for him it was heavy. There is evidence that for more than ten years this burden was upon him. The last receipt was for
groceries, paid for in part by money, in part by
a copy of the "Cyclopædia," in 1862, December 22. The number of claimants was thirty-
three. Of these, seven withdrew. After the
claims had been sifted and all compromises
made, the sums due amounted to a little more
than one thousand dollars.

Mr. Ripley's connection with "The Tribune"
began immediately on the cessation of "The
Harbinger," but was not at first lucrative, for
the paper was still young, having been established in 1841, and a literary department was
not as yet organized. Subsequently the man
made the place, but for several years the journal, afterwards so distinguished as a tribunal of
letters, took a modest position. There was at
this time no such thing as systematic criticism
of literary work in a daily paper. The man
of letters wrote books. Of literary magazines
there were not many. "Harper's New Monthly
Magazine" was ushered into being in 1850; the
first number of "Putnam's Monthly" was issued in January, 1853. The leading writers
were either men of means, or had earned a com
petency by the sale of more ambitious works, —
romances, histories, poems, sketches of travel,

— or were contented to live in retirement without money. Literature, the current literature of the day, the literature which fed the multitude offered but a precarious subsistence, and no hope of fame. In fact, the multitude had no literature deserving the name. There was little general knowledge of books, opinions, or characters. Intelligence was confined to concerns of a material order; the world of thought was not yet open to the many. To earn a livelihood by his pen; and not merely to earn a livelihood, but to pay debts; and not merely to do this, but to create a fame, to erect a standard, and establish a permanent demand for the best thought and the best expression, to make knowledge a public necessity, as it had been a private luxury, was the task which George Ripley accomplished. Not that he contemplated such an achievement when he began; the drift of the time was setting in a literary direction, and gave him opportunities that he could not have anticipated; still he did more than any man to stimulate that tendency, and to him is largely due the substitution of an exact, critical method, in place of the sentimental mood which was earlier in vogue. He wrote from observation, reading, knowledge, not from feeling or fancy. From the first he did this. His training at school and college; his years of experi-

ence in an exacting profession ; his exercise in
reviews and controversies ; his familiarity with
the best productions of American, English, German, and French genius ; the severe mental and
moral discipline of Brook Farm, all conspired
with a remarkable firmness and moderation of
temperament, to repress any impulse towards
affectation or undue exhilaration of judgment,
while his natural buoyancy of spirits, his inborn kindness of heart, his knowledge of intellectual difficulties, and his sympathy with even
modest aspirations, saved him from moroseness,
and rendered it impossible for him to ply with
severity the scourge of criticism.

His earliest experience in journalism was of
the hardest. In the spring of 1849 he moved
to New York from Flatbush. At this time he
spent a few hours daily in the office of " The
Tribune " as " literary assistant," — a " caterer
of intelligence in all languages but the vernacular." He had no leisure for such work as he
wished to do — to review Morell's " Philosophy of Religion," for example ; or Hickock's
" Psychology " for his friend Parker's " Massachusetts Quarterly ; " but " everything is so
overlaid by filigree, spangles, bits of mica, and
so forth in the form of short book notices, correspondence, and other machinery, by which
brain is turned into bread," that he makes ex

cuses for not obliging his dearest friend. Thus he writes on the 9th of July, 1849 : —

MY DEAR THEODORE, — My article on Dr. Bushnell has not got written, and of course not sent. Since I heard from you last I have made a new arrangement with "The Tribune," and now have a regular "bureau" in that office as assistant editor. This so binds me to the flying wings of the daily press, that I can make no engagements of a more responsible character, and of course must forego the satisfaction of being one of your regular contributors. I still hope, however, that I may wake up some fine day and write you an article on some subject purely literary, as I am more and more convinced that theology is beyond my depth. I will make no more promises, and cause no more disappointment.

My present duties are quite to my taste, and give me a moderate livelihood. Ever yours, faithfully,

GEORGE RIPLEY.

What his idea was of a moderate livelihood may be surmised from the following statement, copied word for word from the pay-roll of the paper by one of the officials : —

On the week ending May 5, 1849, Mr. Ripley was paid $5.00 for services on the paper. This is the first time that he appears.

The following week, ending May 12, his name does not appear.

On May 19, the week following, he was paid $5.00.

On May 26, the week following, his name does not appear.

On June 2 he was paid $5.00.

His name does not appear again until June 23, a gap of two weeks, when he was paid $5.00.

On June 30, 1849, he was paid $8.00.

His name does not appear again until July 14, 1849, when he was paid $10.00, and from that date until September 1, 1849, he was paid weekly $10.00.

On September 1, 1849, he was paid $15.00. Thereafter, until April 6, 1850, he received $10.00 per week.

On April 6, 1850, and until September 21, 1851, he received $15.00 per week.

On September 21, 1851, his salary was placed on the pay-roll at $25.00, and remained thus until January 16, 1864, with the exception of the week ending October 4, 1851, when he was paid only $15.00.

On January 16, 1864, he was paid $30.00, and his salary continued $30.00 per week until January, 1866, when it was raised to $50.00, and it remained at that sum until January 11, 1871, when it was raised to the sum of $75.00, and from that time until his death he was paid $75.00 per week for his services.

During his absence in Europe, in 1869, his salary ceased, and he was paid for the letters which he wrote. The sum so paid him was about $30.00 per week. This was done by his own solicitation. He did not wish to receive his regular salary when not at work at the office: but desired to write when he had matter to write about. When he had no subject, or when he did not feel like working, he would not accept of pay.

In connection with the increase of Mr. Ripley's salary in 1871, the following extract from the " Minutes Book " is of interest : —

" Mr. Greeley proposed the following : —

" *Resolved,* That the salary of Mr. George Ripley be increased from $50.00 to $75.00 per week.

"In explanation, he [Mr. Greeley] said that his general opposition to raising the salaries of stockholders was well-known. He thought his own salary had been raised unwisely, and had so said at the time. Raising one salary always incites a claim that half a dozen others should be raised to equalize payment for equal service. He had always opposed, and always would oppose, demands for additional pay based on the needs of the claimant. He did not know whether Dr. Ripley had more or less children than John Rodgers, and did not care. He moved this increase on two distinct and only grounds: I. Dr. Ripley has long served 'The Tribune' industriously and faithfully, and has won a high reputation for its Literary Department. II. He [Mr. Greeley] desired more work of Dr. Ripley than he had hitherto done, and would undertake, if the resolution prevailed, to get the value of the increase out of the Doctor in good honest service."

The resolution was unanimously adopted.

On December 28, 1849, a resolution was passed by the stockholders, in meeting assembled, permitting

Messrs. George Ripley, Samuel Sinclair, and James Cuthill " to purchase stock in the Tribune Newspaper Association," and thereafter they met with the stockholders.

That Mr. Ripley's contributions to the political and miscellaneous columns were no larger, must be explained by the activity of his pen in other directions. A little account book, which has been preserved, contains the names of various periodicals for which he wrote, and even gives the titles of his contributions. They cover the whole field of human interests from social reform to ephemeral amusements; from grave discussions of politics and philosophy to the gossip of the day; the newly-arrived singer; the latest sensation in the dramatic world. He tried his hand at all styles, having an eye to the exigency of the hour. Art, music, opera, concerts, the latest incident in the world of affairs, Kossuth, Jenny Lind, Father Mathew, Miss Bremer, Fanny Davenport, the lecturers, Chapin, Giles, Emerson, the reading of Mrs. Kemble, the Astor Place riot, the Parkman murder, foot-races, Charlotte Cushman, reform and ecclesiastical conventions, the amount of mail matter between Europe and America, spiritual sittings, A. J. Davis and his first big book, the beginning of new literary enterprises, Wordsworth, Allston, the Astor Library, Agassiz, Henry James

Poe, Brownson, Longfellow, Sumner, Garrison, Phillips, Margaret Fuller, Samuel Osgood, Beecher, Macaulay, Bancroft, N. P. Willis, Moses Stuart, Holmes, Thackeray, Horatio Greenough, Comte, Schelling, Nehemiah Adams, James Walker, Daniel Webster, Andrews Norton, Walker's trial for murder, the cholera, the last news from California, the demise of " The True Sun," capital punishment, Friends' Yearly Meeting, the execution of Washington Goode. " Anything but apathy " is his motto. It must be confessed that a finely educated taste like his does not always show to advantage in such promiscuous company. His attempts at success as a penny-a-liner were not examples of brilliant achievement: the lion does not appear well at a menagerie. But the training was excellent, and familiarity with all sorts of literature was valuable. In no other way could he have acquired the discipline needed in his profession.

The breadth of his experience is indicated by the variety of the journals to which he contributed: " The Chronotype," " The Globe," Arthur's "Home Gazette," " The Literary Messenger," " The Washingtonian," " The Picayune." " The Pittsburgh Commercial," " The Columbian," " The Charleston Literary Gazette," " The Manchester Examiner" (English); later

came " The Independent," " Hearth and Home,"
and other periodicals not recorded.   For some
of these he wrote regularly, for others occasionally ; always accommodating his material to the
journal it was prepared for, descanting on books,
politics, travels, the gossip of the day, social
movements, as his readers may have desired.
In several instances the papers were scores in
number, and on every conceivable subject, from
problems of life to the rumors of the streets.
It is bewildering even to note the themes ; and
when it is remembered that all this work was
conscientiously done, was done under serious
difficulties, much of it in hours of fatigue, anxiety, and sorrow, the achievement is astonishing.

In the early period of this labor, the spiritual
earnestness of the man often broke out, as for
example in such language as this : —

" The work of ages goes on ; man advances
nearer to the freedom which is his birthright ;
the temporary evils, that are incidental to all
transitions from an old order of things to a better, pass away, and are forgotten ; the self-sus-
taining, self-recovering power of liberty, insures
the health of the social body ; and in spite of
the Jeremiads of such croaking prophets as M.
Guizot, the serene spirit of humanity unfolds
new strength and beauty in the elastic atmosphere of liberty, until its presence is acknowl
edged universally as benign."

"Gerrit Smith is one of the increasing number, who, with Moses, Jefferson, and Fourier, believe that the monopoly of land is at war with the principles of divine justice; that the usufruct of the earth belongs to the living generations of the race, but its absolute proprietorship to no one but the Creator. This principle is capable of demonstration."

"The Associationists have held several meetings the past week, which have been characterized by an excellent spirit, great union of feeling, and unquenchable devotion to their cause. . . . There is good reason why. They know that the claims they make of social organization are demanded by eternal justice, and will one day be acknowledged by human intelligence."

The literary spirit, temperate, thoughtful, considerate, asserted itself quickly, nor was it long in claiming as its own the whole field of expression. Thus, in February, 1850, he chronicles the beginnings of the Astor Library. His reviews of books and his notices of men contain sketches of character such as none but a master could have produced. Portrait sketches of this time might be multiplied indefinitely, for the rich-minded and warm-hearted writer poured out his impressions with fullness and freedom whenever he reviewed characters or books. His multitudinous productions abound

14

in similar material. Tempting descriptions of
Bancroft, Bushnell, Carlyle, Motley, Mühlen-
berg, Mill, Ruskin, Strauss, Channing, Parker, Büchner, Coleridge, Swinburne, Greeley,
Sainte-Beuve, George Eliot, G. H. Lewes, hang
on the walls of his work-room, done with a few
broad touches by his careful hand. They are
of various dates, but the same conscientiousness
of treatment marks them all. Though not always original, they are always faithfully studied
and honestly executed, without mannerism or
pretense, and always with knowledge derived
from independent study. Several of them im-
plied a large culture in the best schools of literary art ; a few had many years of experienced
thought behind them. To a friend who expressed surprise at the facility with which he
threw off his article on Gœthe, he replied : " It
is not wonderful, seeing that I have been fifty
years about it." He was an illustration of his
own literary principles. In a review of Trench's
" Plutarch " he said : " He who does not write
as well as he can on every occasion will soon
form the habit of not writing well at all." The
mental hospitality finds explanation in another
saying of his : " Exclusive devotion to any object, while it narrows the mental range and contracts, if it does not paralyze, the sympathies,
usually diminishes the causes of temptation."

It must be remembered that all the earlier work was done under severe pressure of care. The writer had none of the luxuries that the man of letters loves. He was poor; he could afford but one room in a boarding-house; his labor was all directed towards the earning of daily bread. He could not pursue his favorite studies, but must compel his mind to take an interest in subjects for which he had no taste. He toiled for bare subsistence; his recreation took the form of toil. He was sustained by his indomitable will, his buoyancy of animal spirits, and the devotion of his wife, who preserved for him, personally, notwithstanding her change of faith, a constant affection. She always saw him go away in the morning with regret, and welcomed his return with joy. She knew that he was toiling for her sake, and was resolved that she would give him such recompense as might be in her power. That he had hours of anxiety and despondency may be easily believed. Without such he would not have been human. But his despondency never got the better of his courage. His moods of depression were largely caused by fatigue, which an excellent constitution enabled him soon to throw off. He possessed an extraordinary capacity for work, and a conscientiousness which was proof against the temptations of indolence and the languors of exhaustion. Work of itself did not fatigue him, partly for the reason, perhaps, that being varied and literary, the pressure was not severely felt on the nerves of sensibility. It was easy to throw from the mind what made no organic part of the mind. Then the even monotony of his labor reduced to a level all but the few very remarkable works which break up at long intervals the plains of the intellectual world.

In 1852, in connection with Bayard Taylor, he compiled a "Handbook of Literature and the Fine Arts," a volume of 650 pages, 12mo, the second in a series of six, projected and published by G. P. Putnam, as a comprehensive cyclopædia for family use. The book, though mainly a compilation, involved much reading and labor. An elaborate article on "Literature," probably from the senior editor's pen, was the most distinguishing feature in it.

When "Putnam's Magazine" was started, in 1853, Mr. Ripley was one of its early contributors. The article on George Bancroft (March, 1853) lays emphasis on the importance of the transcendental school of philosophy, of which Mr. Bancroft was an ardent adherent and an eloquent expositor, pays a warm tribute to "plebeian" institutions, and extols Kant. The article on Horace Greeley (July

1855) regards Mr. Greeley's success as an illustration of American institutions; calls him
a genuine representative of the New England
spirit ; does not fully approve either his political principles or his plans of social reform ;
gives .a fine analysis of his character; casts
a side glance at Mrs. Hemans, as contrasted
with Byron and Shelley, and dwells on the
limitations and infirmities of self-made men.
The paper is brilliant, and not in the least controversial. An article on American literature
(February, 1856) follows Duycinck in the
main ; but contains a warm eulogium on Roger
Williams, as the apostle of soul-freedom. The
paper on Heine (November, 1856) severely
condemns Heine's character ; is rather analyt-
ical and philosophical in tone ; but confines itself pretty closely to the data given in Meiss-
ner's "Erinnerungen." In two articles on
George Sand (February and June, 1857) the
writer follows the course of her "Autobiogra-
phy" without attempting an essay on her genius. There is no bitterness in his comment ;
no rebuke of her "immoralities," only a mild
censure of her eccentricities, and a plea for
charity in respect to her infringements of "the
wholesome regulations of society." The biography of Wm. H. Seward, prefixed to the col-
lective edition of Mr. Seward's works (1853),

was from George Ripley's pen. This, we suspect, was done with enthusiasm, for the writer
was a philosophical democrat, a believer in the
people, at heart in sympathy with all movements aiming at the elevation of the masses.
In a review of Greeley's " Conflict " (" Atlantic Monthly " for July, 1864), he spoke of the
" Compromises of 1850 " as " a monstrous cor-
ruption in legislation, which not even the great
name of Henry Clay could shield from subsequent opprobrium." The following letter from
Charles Sumner proves that long before this was
written George Ripley's name called up associations of reform with literary cultivation : —

BOSTON, *July* 5, 1849.

MY DEAR SIR, — I do not see " The Tribune " habitually, and was not aware till yesterday that there
had been any notice or discussion of anything of mine
in its columns. It is only this evening that I have
seen your most flattering notice. I do not know that
I have ever read any article, mentioning my name,
with more sincere satisfaction than I have just read
that written by you. Knowing your skill as a critic
and your knowledge of the subject [" The Law of
Progress "], I have especial pleasure in your commendation, while I cannot but attribute it in some
measure to a friendly bias, or to the free-masonry
which unites all who are struggling, through the evi.
report of men, for the better time.

I have tried to procure a copy of "The Tribune" containing your notice, but in vain. It was Friday, June 8. I have thought it not impossible that it might be convenient for you to send me a copy of the "Weekly" containing the whole controversy, but I am particularly desirous of preserving your article.

I send you to-day a recent address on "Peace," in which I believe I have shown that great cause to be as practicable as it is beneficent. I have endeavored to disembarrass the question of some of the topics which are sometimes unnecessarily associated with it.

Pardon my free epistle, into which I have been tempted by the exceeding kindness which you have shown to me. Ever faithfully yours,

CHARLES SUMNER.

Mr. Ripley's connection with "Harper's New Monthly Magazine" began with its beginning in 1850, and continued intimate and confidential till his death. He was at first a writer of literary notices for it, but soon took more prominent positions, became a regular contributor, and finally one of its trusted "readers" of works offered to the house for publication or reissue to the American market. The number of the "Opinions" is very great, manuscripts being sent him every week, many of them novels, but many of them works on theological or philosophical themes, volumes of travel, histories, pictures of foreign lands, sketches of char-

acter, essays, narratives of adventure, solid examples of criticism, as well as "airy nothings"
of fancy. To all he gave conscientious examination, not allowing himself to indulge a prejudice in favor of an author or against him, and
keeping in view the interests of literature along
with the expediences of trade. His judgment
was sober, his perception keen, his knowledge
adequate. On his recommendation, many a
good book was sent forth to merited success,
and at his suggestion many a poor one was ar-
rested on its way to the printer. Of necessity,
the judgments were summary and the opinions
short; but the judgments were always well
weighed, and the opinions carefully expressed.
A singular combination of literary sagacity and
worldly wisdom characterized them nearly all.
An author's fame seldom conceals any demer-
its of his work, nor does an author's obscurity
prevent him from bestowing on his production
the attention it deserves. In praising or blam-
ing, he is not contented with wholesale reflections, but limits his approval or his disap-
proval to the qualities he wishes to commend or
to discourage, never failing to distinguish the
special excellence or deficiency of the book under consideration. Such definiteness is a sign
of power; when united with the serenity of
knowledge, it is a sign of remarkable power of

intellect. The writer must confess that a perusal of these "opinions" has impressed upon him the extraordinary mental force of Mr. Ripley, even more than the elaborate reviews which were intended for the public eye, as faithful work done in secret is always more impressive than the most brilliant performance designed to meet the gaze of men. These criticisms, which might easily be expanded into essays, were carelessly thrown to the publisher for his guidance as regarded the availability of commodities for the market, but in truth they are valuable as contributions to literary history. Their close association with the names of authors and the titles of books forbids their publication; except for that, a volume of them would be instructive and medicinal; nutritious to minds in health, curative to minds diseased. The English of them is, of itself, a study, so quiet yet so fair. Mr. Ripley made a conscience of his use of English. He said once, in print, " It is the duty of every educated man to set his face against the innovations which disfigure the language ; to exercise the functions of a committee of vigilance where no verbal tribunal forms a court of final appeal ; and thus to aid in the creation of a body of common law which shall have the force of a statute." So conscientious was he about this, that the most abrupt verdicts, often but two or three lines in length, are expressed in English, not formal or studied, but idiomatic; dashing, yet correct. The "opinions" in question prove the possibility of giving utterance to very strong emotions without departing from the vernacular. "Idiot" and "lunatic" are to be found in the most conservative dictionaries. They who object to Mr. Ripley's gentleness would, perhaps, be of another mind if they could see his written judgment on manuscripts sent to him for inspection.

The "New American Cyclopædia" was begun in 1857. The project was conceived by Rev. Dr. Hawks. Mr. Ripley's connection with the work was coincident with its earliest execution, and the character of the work itself owed much to the patient labor and the unremitting care which he bestowed on it. The publishers, of course, granted every facility, — provided the space for a large corps of workers; supplied the books of reference; paid contributors, sub-editors, purveyors of literary material; did all, in fact, that publishers could do, in affording the "ways and means," — but the success of the undertaking depended much on the manner in which the task was performed, and that rested with the editors, George Ripley and C. A. Dana. They were both busy men; but they were both men of remarkable power of labor and of singular resolution. Both gave their best thought to the enterprise, and as much time as it required. The staff of fellow-laborers was not large at first, but competent writers had charge of the articles; a liberal spirit presided over the undertaking, which, though of gigantic dimensions and formidable responsibility, went on smoothly from week to week. Mr. Ripley himself wrote little or nothing; but the labor of selecting themes and authors, of preserving due proportion of parts, and of correcting errors of statement or of style, was not light. The articles were anonymous; a severe taste excluded individual peculiarities of manner and opinion; a tone purely literary animated every page of the sixteen volumes. The subjects were allotted to the best known authorities, without regard to their ecclesiastical or party connections, and were tried at the tribunal of historical or literary truth before they were admitted. A close and ceaseless watch was kept on every line. Experts in learning passed sentence on each contribution submitted. In fact, no means were left untried to secure, as far as possible, immunity from error. A supplementary volume, published each year, supplied such additions as the progress of events in the old world or the new made necessary, until a complete revision of the whole work was required; but these volumes made no part of the Cyclopædia as being under the care of its editors. The first two or three volumes of the main work were edited solely by Messrs. Ripley and Dana; others, associate editors, came in later, and continued, most of them, till the end.

The first edition was finished in 1862. A complete revision was begun in 1867-68, and completed in less than three years. Though made under the same conditions and auspices as the first, the same editorial care, and, as far as could be, the same critical supervision, it was substantially a new work. Each article was submitted to thorough re-handling; the schedule was reconstructed; much of the old material was dropped; the proportionate length of contributions was altered to suit the increased or diminished importance of subjects; and other writers were called in to make good the places of men whom death had removed, or whom circumstances had rendered unavailable or needless. The new book was a monument of editorial capacity. To it Mr. Ripley gave every hour he could spare from other duties; having it on his mind when it was not on his hands; considering, planning, making notes in his memorandum-book; anxious lest any piece of valuable information should be omitted, or any defective workmanship be admitted; looking after the small details of literary execution, and feeling his way in advance of the contributors that he might not be taken by surprise. Every day found him at his post for several hours, cheerful, buoyant, unresting, and unfatigued, never off his guard, but never petulant. After a pleasant greeting to his fellow-workers he went steadily to work himself, and silence, broken by suppressed murmurs only as questions were asked and answered in an under-tone, reigned throughout the apartment.

Around the editor in chief were ranged his staff. There was Robert Carter, a man of rare and extensive knowledge, for many years connected with the newspaper press, — an editor once and author himself, for a long time correspondent of " The Tribune " at Washington, and a trusted manager of " Appleton's Journal ; " Michael Heilprin, the omniscient, a Hebrew, of Polish extraction, formerly private secretary of Kossuth, — a man of boundless erudition, master of all languages, Eastern and Western, a nice critic of details, especially in history, biography, philology, and geography, since known as the writer of a remarkable work on the history and literature of Israel; Alfred Guernsey, for many years an important servant of the Harpers, conductor of their magazine, chief historian of their well-known " War of the Rebellion;" Francis Teall, whose familiarity with the mysteries of a printing-office made him especially valuable as an inspector and corrector of proofs. Among the revisers were John D. Champlin, Jr., the well-known specialist, historian, and critic; Julius Bing, the industrious literary purveyor; J. R. G. Hassard, the accomplished writer on nearly all subjects R. A. Proctor, the astronomer: in all more than thirty men of more or less literary distinction. With the world's literature beneath them suggesting the patient toil of past centuries, and the roar of traffic in the street outside to remind them of the age to which they belonged, these toilers pursued their unintermitted task of condensing the thought of the generation into form for easy reference. The world was ten years older than it was when the "New American Cyclopædia" began to take the place of the admirable but long obsolete "Encyclopædia Americana." History had made great strides; the globe had yielded up many a secret to modern investigation; philology had unlocked treasures of literature; criticism had reduced ancient prejudices to fictions; charity had pulled down some of the most stubborn barriers of faith; a respect for truth had to some degree taken the place of pride of opinion; it had become in some measure practicable to seek knowledge

where aforetime nothing but ignorance, superstition, and bigotry was looked for, and the mak-
ers of the great Cyclopædia had free permission
to obey the summons.

An abbreviated edition of the work, in four
volumes, was made immediately on the completion of the revision. This was finished two
years before the death of the senior editor.

By agreement with the publishers the two
editors received between them twelve and a half
cents on every volume sold, or one dollar each
on every set. For extra work on the revision
Mr. Ripley was paid two hundred and forty
dollars a month. This began in 1876, and was
continued till the condensed edition in four volumes was finished. The number of volumes
sold of both the large editions, at this date, is
one million four hundred fifty nine thousand
five hundred and fifty; an immense sale, due
in part, no doubt, to the timeliness of the project, in part also to the reputation of the publishers and the well-established fame of the editors in charge.

In 1862, about the time the first edition of the
Cyclopædia was completed, Mr. Ripley formed
a plan for two volumes of papers "selected from
the contributions of the writer to the periodical
press during a long term of years," and even
wrote a preface explaining the contents. The
collection was to be called, -

BOOKS AND MEN.

A SERIES OF
CRITICAL AND BIOGRAPHICAL SKETCHES.
BY GEORGE RIPLEY.

The volumes were never published; the materials for them were probably never selected.
The author was easily diverted from any project of that kind. A native modesty forbade
his attaching importance to the necessarily fugitive productions of his pen. In an age of book-
making he was no book-maker; and besides, his
time was so fully occupied that small leisure
remained for the suitable compilation and edit-
ing of a series like that contemplated. Had
his engagements permitted a careful treatment
of the themes discussed, he might have been
nerved to undertake a work of permanent value,
for which he was well qualified. But there was
little to stir ambition in the plan suggested,
and he never found opportunity to alter it.
With remarkable capacity for authorship, and
more than the common inducements to it in
the form of pecuniary advantage, his standard
of excellence was high. Literature was his mis-
tress, — an exacting one, — whom, in his opinion, he could better serve by the anonymous
daily effort of journalism into which he might
put conscience, knowledge, cultivation, experience, taste, than by any more formal adventure

of authorship. His individual claim to recognition he prized less than the influence which he might exert through the impersonal quality of his mind. This he spent without stint. His friends will acknowledge the dignity of his course, however much they may wish that they possessed some permanent memorial of his activity, or that the world might know its full debt to his faithfulness. Whoso lives for humanity must be content to lose himself. No less than this shall be said here for the man who furnished material for many books, but published none.

15

CHAPTER VI.

GEORGE RIPLEY has now become a man of letters, pure and simple, examining all subjects in a spirit purely literary. Never a dogmatist, never a partisan, never a controversialist, never a theorist or champion of opinions; always an eclectic in the best sense of the term, always a believer in partial but advancing truth, he was now less than ever disposed to commit himself to any school or system. His faith was in thought, his interest was in knowledge, let the thought bear what name it might, let the knowledge proceed from whatsoever quarter. In intellectual passion he was deficient. His heart was warm; his conscience was true; his mind was serene and impersonal. A loyal friend, a faithful citizen, his devotion to truth was dispassionate, for the reason that it was modest. Affection clung to forms; conscience revered visible symbols; but truth was bodiless and eternal. That he dared not limit. That he could only worship from afar. And so strong was his conviction of the claims of intellectual liberty that

to him it would have been nothing short of trea·
son to confine himself within a sect. A theist
he undoubtedly was, a clear, decided one ; but
his theism was wider than any denomination,
broader than any creed. Intolerance, in his
view, was folly. The boldest affirmation was
likely to be nearest to wisdom. His faith might
best be expressed in the lofty language of the
writer of the Apocryphal Book of Ecclesiasti-
cus : " In all ages, entering into holy souls, she
[Wisdom] maketh them to be sons of God and
prophets." Such souls were, in his judgment,
few ; but he revered them wherever found, and
he found them in all communions. In a review
of Mr. Mallock's volume, " Is Life Worth Living ? " he wrote, " The consciousness of a spiritual life has not passed away from a host of
minds of profoundest thought, who find nothing
in the disclosures of science to shake their faith
in the eternal verities of reason and religion."
Later (1879), reviewing Arnold's " Light of
Asia," he said, " As an exposition of the relig·
ious system of Buddha we reckon this poem as
no more successful than the numerous similar
attempts in prose. We have no sufficient data
for the solution of the problem. But as a magnificent work of imagination and a sublime appeal in the interests of the loftiest human virtue, we tender it the sincerest welcome, and

grasp the author by the hand as a genuine prophet of the soul." In a notice of Kiddle's "Spiritual Communications," printed about the same time, he writes: "The book affords a fearful example of the danger of substituting the suggestions of personal fancy for the universal principles of morality, and the practical rules for the conduct of the understanding, which have been accepted in all civilized communities."

He was too well acquainted with schools of philosophy to commit himself without reserve to either, and too familiar with creeds to repeat any with full conviction. Having personal friendships with men and women of all persuasions, he preserved his mental integrity without restricting his social intercourse; in fact, the completeness with which he kept his private faith enabled him to maintain his social intercourse; for it was quite well understood that he was purely a man of letters, whose impersonality of opinion made bigotry impossible on his part, and disarmed the spirit of proselytism in others. He met nobody on the dogmatical plane; on the intellectual plane he cordially met anybody. He was never heard to pray, he was never heard to say his catechism; he was never heard to make confession of sin. Yet who dares to say he was wanting in humility? The books he loved to read were books

on physiology. Yet he was no materialist, but
an idealist to the end of his days. No church
could claim him, but no church could disclaim
him ; and in hours of intimacy, when the veil
was removed from his spirit, his discourse took
tone of solemnity which could belong only to
one who stood near the dividing line between
the temporal and the eternal, and was keenly
sensitive to the lightest breath of moral or spiritual skepticism. To Theodore Parker, in
1852, he wrote: " I regard Schleiermacher as
the greatest thinker who ever undertook to
fathom the philosophy of religion. If he had
only placed his ' Infinite ' in the human soul he
would have come upon the right track, shad-
owed forth by the ' $\delta\alpha\iota\mu\omega\nu$ ' of Socrates, the ' To
$\Theta\epsilon\acute{\iota}o\nu$ ' of Plato, the ' O $\Theta\epsilon o\varsigma$ $\epsilon\sigma\tau\iota$ $\pi\nu\epsilon\upsilon\mu\alpha$ ' of Christ,
and whatever else acknowledges the God with-
in us, or theism against atheism. In this faith
we have a grand comprehensive reconciliation."
The atheistical theory, however set forth, had
no attraction for him. " I have read but little
of Feuerbach. He seems crabbed and dogmatic in his atheism, and can have little influence, I presume, except on the confirmed sys-
tem-lover."

The following extracts from printed judgments may fitly be cited here as indicating the
cast of his thought on religious themes : —

[*Büchner's Man in the Past, Present, and Future.*]

Among the physiologists of the extreme material
istic school, Dr. Büchner has gained a certain degree
of celebrity by the freedom of his speculations and
the audacity of his theories, rather than by any pretensions to accuracy of learning or soundness of judgment. The present work, like the productions by
which he is already known to the public, bears the
marks of crude and superficial reflection; its method is
loose and desultory, its reasonings are plausible rather
than convincing, and its statements appear to aim at
popular effect rather than at precision and exactness
of information or sobriety of inference. As a writer,
Dr. Büchner has no mastery of ease or elegance of
expression; his sentences are framed after the most
confused models of German construction, and the
lack of flow and neatness in his style makes the perusal of his disquisitions more of a task than a pleasure. The interest of this volume consists in being
one of the latest, and, in some respects, one of the
most complete, accounts of the results of modern research with regard to the physical history and development of the human race.

[*Mallock on Modern Skepticism.*]

The present work, "Is Life worth Living," like
the previous productions of the author, indicates an
excess of imagination over clearness of insight and
soundness of judgment. His fancy takes alarm at
the portentous shapes which are dimly descried

through the mist of a mirage, instead of his patiently examining their proportions in the veracity of sunlight. His description of modern science, in many respects, must be regarded as a caricature, of which the colors have been supplied by the intensity of his fears rather than by the tranquil observation of facts. It is certain that the men of science of the present day are not tinctured with the spirit of unbelief to the extent which is represented by the author. The successors of Faraday and Agassiz, who share their faith while they inherit their science, are by no means few in number or narrow in influence. The consciousness of a spiritual life has not passed away from a host of minds of profoundest thought, who find nothing in the disclosures of science to shake their faith in the eternal verities of reason and religion. Nor, perhaps, is the present age more deserving the name of an age of unbelief than preceding ages. The eighteenth century presented an example of denial and doubt, of profane scoffing and dissolute living, to which no parallel can now be found; but it was succeeded by a more passionate love of truth, a higher tone of ethics, and a deeper sense of religion. If the reign of dogma has been weakened, the dominion of a spiritual faith has gained fresh power and won wider triumphs.

Mr. Mallock's book, accordingly, affords a curious example of taking a part for the whole, of overlooking a wide circle of social and human interests, of ignoring large classes of profound and powerful thinkers, of taking for granted the death of religious

faith, as he witnessed the obsequies of certain temporary forms.   The dirge-like notes with which he ac-
companies the procession will not be accepted as the
music of humanity, nor will the burial of the soul
be deemed the inevitable result of the progress of science.

[*William E. Channing.*]

. . . His integrity of purpose was equally conspicuous in his convictions and in his doubts.   Next
to his love of humanity, his most ardent passion was
the love of truth, if it was not his love of truth
which inspired his profound devotion to the interests
of humanity.   He had no taste and little capacity for
controversy.   He delighted in the comparison of ideas,
especially with men whose earnestness and good faith
inspired him with confidence in their intentions ; but
the atmosphere of strife and debate was not congenial with his feelings, and prevented the free exercise
of his highest faculties.   There was almost a child-
like simplicity in his mind, which, in spite of perhaps
an excessive self-consciousness, led him to listen
meekly to suggestions, even from the humblest quar-
ters, and to maintain the attitude of an inquirer rather
than a teacher.   He had no tincture of a dogmatic
spirit.   He was suspicious of broad generalizations
tracing their origin to imagination and eloquence
more often than to accurate research, and hence was
always disinclined to the adoption of a system.   He
rejoiced in every glimpse of truth which was opened
to his sight, but never presumed that he had ex

Theism.

The vital question of modern inquiry relates to the first principle and origin of existence. Every movement of thought is but the effort of the mind to grasp the individual facts of nature in a comprehensive unity, and to interpret the universe according to the suggestions of reason. In all ages men have attempted an ideal construction of natural phenomena. But they have never been able to rest in anything short of an absolute unity: a unity which is the negation of all plurality and change; a unity which is unconditioned itself, and yet conditions everything; an eternal constancy, which produces all geneses and all variety. Thinkers have always apprehended, with more or less clearness, that the first principle must be one or nothing. This is tacitly conceded in all modern systems of thought. On this ground Büchner the materialist, Spencer the dynamist, Hegel the idealist, Cousin and Coleridge the spiritualists, meet in common. The ultimate problem of all philosophy is to determine the relation of human thought to this absolute principle. Among the solutions of the problem there are four distinct types, which, in the opinion of the author, exhaust the discussion. First, it has been maintained that matter, with its essential attribute of force, explains the origin of the universe. Second, the absolute principle has been found in force, considered as the cause of all the manifold phenomena of the universe. Third, thought has been assumed as an eternal process of evolution, forming the supreme principle of all reality.

Fourth, the causative principle of existence and phenomena is an unconditioned will, a living and personal Being, determining all the conditions of the universe with reference to a final purpose. The first and second of these systems are essentially the creeds of atheism; the third is that of pantheism; the fourth, that of theism.

In the summer of 1848 his wife dropped her teaching at Flatbush. Late in the autumn of that year they came to New York. About that time, either immediately before or immediately after their removal, she professed her faith in Romanism. Tired and disappointed, her illusions dispelled, her enthusiasm exhausted, —

> Weary of herself, and sick of asking
> What she was and what she ought to be, —

she sunk, like a spent child, into her nurse's arms. " I have found my mother," was her cry. The conversion must have been a grief to her husband; but if it was he did not betray it. This change of faith made no division between them. Whatever lack of mental and spiritual correspondence it may have occasioned, it caused no break of private sympathy, no withdrawal of affectionate respect. They honored and loved each other as before. He appreciated her devotion, aided her charities, took an interest in her occupations, rejoiced in her happiness, humored what to him seemed her fancies. Their social delights they shared together. Agreeing not to talk on questions of religious opinion, they were quite free to communicate on other subjects, and never allowed any root of bitterness to spring up and trouble them. They were seen together in public, and in private were the delight of a select circle of friends. Their lot was humble, but their hearts were light. Her days were consecrated to offices of piety and love; his were spent in the drudgery of literature. Hers were passed among the poor and friendless of the metropolis; his in his office, among his books. But in the evening they met and conversed cheerily, as if neither was preoccupied.

In 1859, while stooping to pick up some article which had fallen behind her dressing-table, she struck against the sharp corner of the marble top with such violence that the pain obliged her to sit down till she could recover herself. She said nothing about it, but soon afterward noticed a hard lump in the right breast, at the bruised spot; still she said nothing. In June, 1860, Mr. Ripley being called to Greenfield to the death-bed of his brother Franklin, she consulted a physician, who was shocked at the progress of disease. Still she said nothing to her husband till two days after his return, when, on his remarking that he had dispatched the work which had accumulated in his absence, she threw out a hint of her condition. It was too late. There was an operation, she apparently recovered, was happy, gentle, sweet, and so merry that it was a joy to see her. In October they made a little journey to Boston and Greenfield. But in November the suffering returned, and went on increasing in severity until the end, in February, 1861. The agony was intense, but the patience was saint-like; the serenity of spirit was unbroken. No murmur escaped the lips; no expression of impatience added to the grief of those about her; her thoughts were not for herself, but for those whose pain she could do nothing to relieve. Her faithful husband did for her all that was in his power: sat by her, consoled her, cheered, procured every alleviation his means would allow, administered with his own hand the soothing draught, was comforter, nurse, physician, most tender and thoughtful of friends. They had but one room. His writing-table was in one corner, and there he sat at work, night after night and day after day, his brain reeling, his heart bleeding, his soul suspended on her distress. So it went on for three months. A kind friend in the house said at last: "Occupy our rooms to-night; my wife and I will go to a hotel." That night was her last. Her husband told his sister he could have shouted for joy to think that the agony was over.

The funeral was celebrated with all possible circumstance, in fullest accordance with the rite of the Roman Church, with music and priestly vestments, as the authorities desired and as affection prompted. The remains were taken to Boston. Prayers were said in the old Purchase Street meeting-house, then a Catholic church, — he sitting where she sat in years gone by, her body occupying the place of the ancient communion-table. At his instance, ground was consecrated for her resting-place in the old cemetery at Cambridge. The pale, bloodless man went back to a cold fireside.

With the death of his wife, George Ripley's life seemed to be at an end. She represented his whole past. She had been his intellectual companion during the studious years of his ministry; she had shared his visions of the new earth; she had borne her part cheerfully in the labors of Brook Farm; she had aided his efforts to build up a new home in another city; she had endeared herself to his soul by her fortitude during a terrible sickness; she was consecrated by the experience of death. Her departure left him not only alone, but lonely and depressed. He went from New York to Brooklyn, where he lived in retirement for several months.

The following note to his niece well describes his condition at this period: —

New York, *June* 26, 1861.

MY DEAR NIECE, — The month of June has al
most gone, and I have not yet replied to your very
kind note, inviting me to spend a few days with you in
Greenfield before the close of the delightful month.

But I must not yield to the temptation which you
place in my way; at present I have neither health
nor spirits which would make me a welcome guest,
even with the nearest relatives; and I am so tied
down with expediting the publication of our thirteenth
volume, to make up for the delay of the last two,
that I cannot leave my post without great incon-
venience, although I must manage to get a few days
some time in July, which I have long promised to
my Boston friends. This must be the extent of my
visiting for the summer, but perhaps the pleasant
autumn days may entice me out of my solitude to
look again on your beautiful hills and meadows.

I beg you to give my kind remembrances to your
brother Franklin, and my affectionate regards to my
new niece, whose acquaintance I shall look forward
to making with pleasure. If they should be in New
York during the summer, or at any other time, I shall
depend on being informed of their arrival, and shall
rejoice to do anything in my power (little, indeed, at
the best) to make their visit agreeable. Marianne
pent last Sunday week with me at Brooklyn, and
on Monday I went with her to her green retreat at
Morrisania. It is a perfectly rural place, abounding
with shrubbery and flowers, and with a pleasant out
look on the forest. She seems quite contented in

her new home, and I have no doubt that the change of air and scene will do her good.

With my love to your mother, and kind regards to any of my relatives you may chance to see,

I remain ever your affectionate friend and uncle,

G. R.

From this seclusion he emerged in many respects an altered man; affable and courteous as ever, winning in manner, sweet in disposition, but silent as to his former life. To the outside observer, the casual acquaintance, the temporary friend, the ordinary associate of the office or the parlor, he seemed light-hearted, chatty, companionable. They did not see or know what an abyss of memory lay hidden beneath the charming verdure of his conversation, and perhaps thought that he had ceased to think of what he did not disclose. A deep reserve forbade the intrusion of profane eyes, and he passed through the rest of his life a man little comprehended and for the most part misunderstood. Naturally, he, being now alone and of a social disposition, went into society more than he was used to, saw more people, sought more the companionship and solace derived from intercourse with congenial friends, who never found him dull or self-absorbed. Still his solitary hours were many. The fires were not extinguished; the embers still were glowing;

16

but a thick layer of ashes concealed them from view, and he suffered no breath but his own to blow it off, or waken the brands to flame.

Leaving Brooklyn, he returned to New York to live quietly in his literary tasks, in the society of a few secluded friends, and the musings of his own heart. His week-days were passed in the toil of an exacting calling; on Sunday he did not fail to be in his place at the church whose ministrations carried him back nearest to the associations of his youth.

CHAPTER VII.

THE NEW DAY.

THUS the uneventful years went on. His labors became more concentrated; his engagements less distracting. The Cyclopædia was
finished. Work had wrought upon him a sav-
ing, healing, consoling influence. He took a
wider range of relaxation ; he went more freely
abroad. One evening, at the house of a friend,
he met the lady who opened to him the prospect
of a new career. She was German by birth,
and Parisian by education ; well born, well connected ; amiable ; a favorite among her friends,
respected by all who knew her, attractive in
person and manner. She was a widow, having
made an unfortunate marriage in Germany,
which had been terminated in New York; then,
rather than go back to her father's house, where
she was greatly desired, she preferred to maintain herself, in America, as a teacher of music,
which was one of her accomplishments. She
was younger than Mr. Ripley by thirty years,
— so much younger, in fact, that he proposed at
first to adopt her as his daughter, doubting if

he could ever marry again. This arrangement being impracticable, he made her his wife. The marriage took place in the autumn of 1865, and, it is not too much to say, disclosed to him a new life. It withdrew him from his seclusion; brought him into the social world; carried him for the first time to Europe; threw him into relations with eminent people in the scientific and literary circles of foreign lands; enlarged the sphere of his intellectual sympathy; and, in a word, introduced him to another order of men and women. From this point his career as a public man may be said to have begun. He was, as before, a man of letters, but his power as a man of letters was more widely acknowledged, if not more extensively felt. He spent as much time as ever at his desk, perhaps more; but his hours of solitude were fewer. Society occupied them, bringing the relief of change and the stimulus of new thoughts. Contact with his kind quickened his intellectual force. His sympathies expanded, and while the Puritan austerity of his character did not relax, the cordiality of his attitude towards all sorts and conditions of men was more decidedly marked. He seemed more worldly because his world was larger. A letter to his sister belongs to this period : —

NEW YORK, *February* 25, 1866.

MY DEAR MARIANNE, — We were delighted to receive your kind letter of February 4, but we have both of us been in such constant whirl of social engagements that writing has seemed pretty much out of the question. We still continue to have a great many invitations, and the accepting of the same and making calls in return absorb almost every hour of leisure, and we seldom have an evening at home. Lent at last brings a little respite, and I begin to think that it is quite a necessary, if not a beautiful, institution. In spite of everything, however, I have written more for "The Tribune" since November 1 than ever before. My articles appear regularly every Thursday in the Daily, making nearly a page always, and never less than four columns; but it is often some time before they appear in the Semi-Weekly or Weekly, if they get in at all. I do write a good deal for "The Independent," and have had long articles there on Robertson's Memoirs, Bushnell on the Atonement, and Archbishop Hughes's Life.

I have decided to go to Europe about the last of April, to remain till the middle of October. We think of sailing from Boston, making our visit there the week previous, and would like to spend a day or two in Greenfield on the way, if it would n't put the folks out there, with the idea of being obliged to entertain us. M. E. is very kind and affectionate, and seems to take a great interest in her new relative, whom I am sure she will admire very much when she comes to know her. With kindest remembrances to all the B.'s.   Yours ever truly,   G. R.

His first visit to the Old World was made in the summer of 1866, the season of the short, sharp war between Prussia and Austria, an account of which he wrote in letters to " The Tribune," distinguished by the fullness and accuracy of their information, as well as by sagacious observation of the sentiments of brotherhood which were beginning to stir the heart of the German people, and portended their eventual unity. His wife's relations in Stuttgart put him in the way of intelligence on this subject; it was the talk of the dinner-table, and the papers in the excellent reading-room were full of it. The following letters to his sister tell the story of his travels and the condition of his mind in words of his own. His journal records the effect which the first view of the Alps made on his mind: " It was singularly impressive and suggested profound reflection. But to me it was no place for the study of natural theology, to which use it is often applied; the question of absolute causation found no answer here; I was struck with the whole as a wonderful display of the physical forces of the universe. Obvious law and order, however, were wanting. The spectacle reminded me of nature in some grim frolic or terrible convulsion, rather than of the serene and fruitful harmonies which stamp the eternal Cosmos."

STUTTGART, *September* 13, 1866.

MY DEAR MARIANNE, — On returning here on
the 1st instant from our August tour in Switzerland
and Italy, I found your good letter of August 13,
which gave us both great pleasure. We had a truly
delightful month in traveling : the weather, almost
without exception, was perfect, the accommodation
on the road excellent, and the journey throughout
filled with scenes of novelty and splendor. After
sending the little Carmela [daughter of Mrs. R. by
the former marriage] and her nurse to Stuttgart, we
left Baden-Baden on the 1st of August for Switzerland. Since that time I have written nothing for
" The Tribune." Now that the war is over I could
find little to write about that would interest our readers ; for although the objects one meets with in traveling are full of excitement to the observer, they have
been described so often that they seem like an old
story. On leaving Baden, in the northwest corner of
Switzerland, I was trudging up a steep hill to see the
ancient cathedral, when who should I meet but my
friend C. T. Brooks, the Unitarian minister of New-
port, and the translator of Goethe and Richter, whom
you must know by reputation, if not personally. The
rencontre was quite unexpected and very agreeable,
and I took it as a good omen on our entrance into
Switzerland. Our next stage was Neuchâtel, passing
Lake Bienne, which is bordered for miles with luxuriant vineyards, in which we could distinguish the
rich clusters of almost ripe grapes. At Neuchâtel,
which is situated on a lake of the same name, we had

our first distinct view of the Alps, giving us a fore-
taste of the mountain scenery, which proved so grand
and often so terrific on a nearer acquaintance. From
Neuchâtel we proceeded to Geneva, passing through
Yverdon, the seat of Pestalozzi's famous experiments in education; Lausanne, where Gibbon com
posed his immortal history; and Coppet, where was
the residence of Madame de 'Staël, during her ban
ishment from Paris by Napoleon. We then went up
the Lake of Geneva to Vevey, and, turning our faces
once more to the North, proceeded through Freyburg
to Berne, the capital of the Swiss Confederacy.
Here we met Parke Godwin and his family, who
sailed about a month before us, and have been passing the summer in Switzerland. Our next movement
was to Thun, and up the lake of that name to Inter-
lachen, one of the most romantic spots in the alpine
valleys. From here we made excursions to Lauter-
brunnen, the Staubbach Falls, and the glaciers of
Grindelwald. The next day we crossed a branch of
the Alps by the Brünig Pass to Lucerne, and had
our first experience of the wonderful alpine roads,
which are among the greatest triumphs of civil engineering in the world. The path has often been
gained by cutting through the solid rock, making a
platform, or rather a shelf, for the carriage on the
side of a precipice. We look down upon the awful
depths below; but the road is so guarded with strong
parapets that all sense of danger is lost. The scenery is at once majestic and beautiful. Frequent wa-
terfalls rush down the side of the mountain, gloomy

heights tower above, while meadows of the softest green and richest vegetation repose in the distant valleys at our feet. During our stay at Lucerne we made an excursion on the celebrated lake, and visited the scenes of the famous legends in the history of William Tell. The scenery in this quarter is as remarkable in its kind as any in Switzerland, and made a deep impression. Here we made the acquaintance of a charming English family named Egremont, consisting of the widow of a clergyman and her two daughters. They took a great fancy to Louisa, and made themselves very agreeable by their simple, kind-hearted manners, and their refined and intelligent conversation. At Lucerne we also received a visit from my old friends Mrs. Professor Robinson (Talvi) and her daughters, from New York, who, since the death of Dr. Robinson, have resided mostly in Europe. They called, however, while we were out, and as we had not time to return the visit we did not see them.

We now turn our steps towards the east of Switzerland, and by way of Zug, Zürich, and Lake Wallenstadt proceed to Ragatz and Coire. Here we take a private carriage for a three days' journey over the Alps to Lake Como, by the famous Splügen Pass, and commence the most interesting portion of our tour. We were accompanied by an Italian gentleman, an old friend of my wife and her family, whom we met at Baden, and whose experience we thought would be of service to us in traveling in Italy. I can give no idea of the wonderful road over the al-

pine heights, especially the stupendous Via Mala,
where a path is hewn out between two precipices
30 feet from each other, and between 500 and 600
feet above the Rhine, which forces itself through
the rocky bed as a narrow, roaring rivulet. Lake
Como, which we have traversed from end to end,
presents a striking contrast in its quiet loveliness,
and the smiling fields and beautiful villas on each
side. Thence we proceeded to Milan (noblest of
cities), Turin, Alessandria, Genoa, Parma and Mo-
dena, Bologna, Florence, Pisa, and Leghorn. We
did not think it prudent to extend our journey to
Rome and Naples, as the weather was growing very
hot, and the season for malarial fever and other dis-
eases was at hand. The military occupation of the
railroads, near the seat of war, also prevented us from
fulfilling our intention of visiting Venice. On that
account we were able to make a longer stay at Bologna (the native place of our Italian friend) and at
Milan, as lovely a city, I am sure, as all the kingdoms of the earth can show. It was time to retrace
our steps, and, proceeding up the delicious Lake Mag-
giore, we crossed the Alps in a diligence at night by
the Bernhardin Pass, and, stopping at Friedrichshafen
(where the King of Würtemberg has a rural residence) and Ulm, we arrived safe and happy at Stuttgart on Saturday, September 1st. We found Carmela
and the family well and delighted to see us again,
and our stay proves so agreeable that we decide to
remain here till the 16th, and then go directly to
Paris, instead of leaving on the 10th for the Rhine,

Cologne, and Brussels, as we had intended. We ex
pect to remain in Paris about a fortnight, spending
only a day or two in England previous to sailing in
the Scotia, October 6th. I shall hope to be in New
York about the 16th, and shall be very glad to find a
letter from you at the Tribune office, as there will
be no time to receive one at Liverpool before we
sail. I have written to Mr. T., who takes charge of
my affairs in my absence, to engage us temporary
lodgings at the Fifth Avenue Hotel; but beyond that
I have made no arrangement for the winter. After
the quiet and beautiful domestic life which we have
enjoyed for so great a part of the summer, the prospect of a New York boarding-house is anything but
delightful, and I confess that I feel a little dismayed
at the enormous expense which is involved for such
comparatively unsatisfactory returns. The mode of
life in Europe is generally far more simple than with
us, especially among people of moderate circumstances, although more real elegance and incomparably more comfort can be obtained at the same cost
than in New York or Boston. I do not wonder that
so many Americans prefer a long residence in Europe from motives of economy, although for myself,
with pursuits so decidedly American, I am not
tempted to follow their example. It will be a great
sacrifice to me, as well as to her mother, to leave behind the little Carmela. She is the most faultless and
charming child that you can imagine, with an uncom-
monly fine intellect, a most affectionate and loving disposition, and a beauty of character beyond her years

But she is so much better off here than she could be in New York that we do not hesitate for a moment. Her grandparents, moreover, who love her more than if she were their own child, would never consent to part with her, and as they have brought her up as their own for more than six years their claim cannot be disputed. She is in the very best social circles in Europe; all her surroundings leave nothing to be desired. She is in one of the best schools in Germany, and, with a private governess and accomplished masters in every special branch, will receive an education that, with my limited means, it would be impossible to give her in America. With everything that wealth and affection and the highest social standing among those with whom her life will probably be passed can impart, I think it would be folly and selfishness on our part to insist on taking her with us to America, where it is no easy matter to establish and maintain a comfortable home for ourselves.

I am not surprised that you decided to remain so long in Madison. As long as you can keep a contented mind there, perhaps you are better off than you could be in Massachusetts. After the departure of S—— B——, you will not have much to interest you, taking it for granted that Mrs. A—— and her daughter will be in the vicinity of Boston. I am glad you find so kind and intelligent a friend in W—— K——, although I have little faith in any attempts to promote Liberal Christianity in the West. Nearly thirty years ago I went over the whole ground, and, from personal observation from Albany to Chicago, became satisfied that during the present age the prospects of religious progress in that quarter would not be brilliant. The people are too secular, too little inclined to study and reflection, too much absorbed in business and politics, to appreciate the serene and beautiful spirit of pure Christianity.

I saw the other day, in an American newspaper, some account of the will of my old comrade, J. H., who, it seems, died worth nearly half a million. He had just graduated as a charity scholar at Cambridge when I first saw him; afterwards became a professor, then a railroad engineer, and married Mrs. F., and that is about the last I ever heard of him. Pray tell me all you know about it. I fear you will hardly have patience to read this long yarn, and will be glad that Louisa is so taken up with visitors that she is not able to write this time. With kind regards from her and me to Mr. B. and family,

I am truly yours,   G. R.

NEW YORK, *November* 1, 1866.

MY DEAR MARIANNE, — I take it for granted that you have received my letter of some ten days since, announcing our safe return. We have taken very pleasant lodgings, No. 122 Madison Avenue, in a private family, with only six or eight other boarders, and consider ourselves quite fortunate in having been able to make arrangements for the winter so speedily and so agreeably. The price, however, is so far in advance of my means and plans, that, as soon as I can find a more suitable shelter, I shall not fail to do so.

Since my return I have not had leisure to turn round, much less to write anything but what was strictly necessary in my daily tasks, which I resumed a week ago last Monday. I have constant visits, both at the house and office, which consume my time, and make the days and evenings all too short. Augusta, as we generally call her now, is warmly welcomed home by our friends, both old and new. She is still troubled with a cough, but she is looking remarkably well, and I trust the cough is not of a serious nature, although it has now hung on for several months. A few years ago she suffered in a similar way from the effect of the Brooklyn air, and was obliged to remove to New York, but was at last cured by the use of cod-liver oil. She is very happy in our new lodgings, and likes New York better than I do, although she is naturally a little homesick at times after the dear little Carmela and her parents, who love her so much. But she makes friends of all who know her.

I have written much more than I expected to do when I began, and hope to receive an answer soon. Don't think me indifferent to the progress of Liberal Christianity in the West. I only suggested some obstacles from my own experience; but no doubt great changes have taken place since I was there.

Ever yours,   G. R.

New York, *February* 12, 1867.

My dear Marianne, — I have both your letters of January 18th and 28th, but, as usual, have been so busy as not to be able to find a moment for writing in reply. "The Tribune," in its enlarged form, gives me more space than heretofore, and as a rule I have two or three columns twice a week, usually on Thursdays and Saturdays, besides a column of literary items on Monday, which it is a good day's work to prepare. I also find it convenient to do whatever extra work I can find, and at present contribute a good deal to "The Independent," which "The Springfield Republican" says is edited by infidels and Unitarians. In last week's paper, the articles on Parton's "Webster," N. P. Willis, and Victor Cousin were mine, though without my name. I have other articles on hand, and shall continue to write from time to time, so you see my pen has to keep jogging on in the old track, and leaves me little leisure for anything else. We are not visiting quite so much as last winter. Augusta still suffers from a cough, and is not able to go out often in the evening, and, unless the weather is pleasant, she stays in the house all day. She had an attack of bronchitis three years ago, and has coughed more or less ever since. In other respects she has excellent health, is always in fine spirits.

We had very pleasant letters last week from Stuttgart, from Mr. and Mrs. Horner, little Carmela, her governess, and from an old friend of my wife's, formerly her governess, now living at Baden-Baden, where we saw her in July. Carmela writes me a letter in English, in which she is making rapid and good progress, and I trust will speak it as well as German by the time we see each other again. She is a sweet, loving child, very attractive in all her ways, and without any apparent fault. We are both homesick for her always, but I would not on any account have her in our rough-and-tumble city until she is a good deal older than she is now. She is now in a quiet, domestic atmosphere, with every possible advantage for education and health, and, although petted by her grandparents, seems to be entirely unspoiled. She is very fond of her " papa and mamma," and with her artless and affectionate nature wins the love of all who know her. I forgot whether I told you that she has taken my name, and is now called Carmela Ripley.

I rather regret that a small annual sum could not be provided for our sister during the short time that she will probably remain with us; as in that case I should be able not only to make a liberal contribution, but to supply any deficiency, so that she should not have the fear of want, which is really worse than actual poverty, as long as she lives. As it is, I presume that I can occasionally do enough, with my limited means, to keep her from suffering, although it is incomparably more to my taste to have a fixed and regular arrangement than to leave such things in uncertainty. I sent her $100 the first of February, which I hope will do for the present; but should you learn in any way that there is need of more, you must not hesitate to inform me. We cannot be too thankful that the enterprising Rachel did not persuade her to join the wild-goose Jaffa scheme, which she was strangely inclined to do a year ago. . . . It was quite an adventure for you to go up to the grand Sanhedrim at Milwaukee, and I am sure you must have enjoyed it very much. I am happy to hear such good accounts of Mr. Kimball; your interest in him and in his religious plans is better for you than any medicine, though I do not advise you to take Liberal Christianity as a drug. He is evidently one of the offshoots of the great banian-tree planted by Theodore Parker, which take root wherever they find a congenial soil, and bring forth abundance of beautiful and wholesome fruit. What a treat it was to you, to be sure, to meet the seraphic R. W. E. away up there in your ends of the earth! I have seen him several times within a year, — this winter, just before he started for the West. I really think he grows softer and more human in his old age. With kindest love from Augusta and me to the family,

Ever yours faithfully, G. R.

The enjoyment derived from this visit, the sense of refreshment after so many years of wearing toil, the feeling of mental expansion, of elation, arising from an extended intercourse with nature and men, naturally made him wish to visit Europe again, more at his leisure; accordingly, in the spring of 1869 he made arrangements for a more comprehensive tour,

17

embracing London, the abode of so many men of power in science, philosophy, and literature and Italy, which was to be the scene of the ecclesiastical Council designed to reanimate the faith, unite the sympathies, and quicken the zeal of Catholic Christendom. The experiences of this trip are recorded in a series of remarkable letters to "The Tribune," too long to be printed in full, and too solid to be abbreviated. The first is dated "at sea, May 20th." Mr. Ripley enjoyed the ocean voyage, the leisure, the opportunity for random reading, the easy, various society, the stir of life among the sailors, the aspects of water and sky. He had no suffering from sea-sickness, was happy and companionable, full of practical wisdom, without assumption or pretense. He was but ten days in London, at the height of the season, too; his pockets filled with letters of introduction to distinguished people, whom he was interested to see; his mind teeming with new suggestions, and alive to all impressions of genius in individuals and in the people. Every hour, consequently, was occupied. The description of Derby Day was written in London, May 27th, but it was not till he reached Baden-Baden, in the middle of July, that time was allowed for a tranquil review of his exciting visit to the metropolis of the world. The usual objects which attract the stranger are passed by without notice: the Tower, the ancient city, the historic houses, streets, squares; the Temple, the Monument, the relics of antique grandeur, the Museum, the public and private picture-galleries, the art collections, the theatres, clubs, concerts, parks, gardens, palaces, receive no attention. He is absorbed in the study of human nature in its actual condition, the physical and mental peculiarities of the people, the state of society, efforts to reform abuses, popular habits and tastes, movements towards harmony in trade and religion, currents of opinion among scientific men of all orders, tendencies of speculation in the world of thought, the men and women whose names were associated with intellectual advance, the prospects of civilization in its higher aspirations. Two or three extracts from a not very copious and somewhat too personal journal for public eyes will give an idea of his alertness of mind: —

Wrote a note to Prof. Jowett, asking permission to pay my respects to him, as a prominent man in the English movement for a more liberal theology. Had a very gracious reception. Talked of Emerson, T. Parker, Frances Power Cobbe, with whom he has entire sympathy, and Bunsen. Touched on President Johnson and American politics generally. Sound in

Northern faith. He is a mild, pleasant-looking man, of about forty-five, of brisk, lively manners (perhaps not unlike Dr. Bushnell), quite free from affectation, and an agreeable, unpretending talker. English in his tones and ways. Cake and wine on the table, which he offered me, but I did not partake. He keeps bachelor's hall in a spacious suite of rooms, elegant but not splendid. Very comfortable and home-looking, — a mode of life which every true student might envy. Celibacy is common in Oxford, but by no means universal even among the Fellows. Cultivated to a high degree, and with excellent taste, his better instincts prompt him to seek a more liberal theology than that of the Church, but he is a follower of leading minds, not a path-finder. Probably inferior to Colenso in boldness and sagacity, certainly in practical influence.

Impressed with the commercial greatness and power of London. Admirable physique of the people. Emerson's description true to the life. Prevailing ignorance beyond a certain line. Great order and external morality in the streets.

I like very much to witness the displays of human strength. Whether physical or intellectual, the spectacle is amost equally interesting. The sight of organized labor has a perpetual charm.

Called on John Bright, Herbert Spencer, Louis Blanc, W. H. Channing. None at home but Louis Blanc. A keen, black-eyed, vivacious Frenchman full of fire and enthusiasm, demonstrative in his manner, and eloquent in his discourse. He speaks English correctly, but with a strong French accent, uses much gesture, and declaims rather than talks. He commands the language more easily in its rhetorical forms than in familiar conversation. He seems to be born for a political orator, and should be in the legislature. We talked of French and American politics, on which he gave an elaborate dissertation. His bearing is earnest and affectionate, too expressive for common occasions.

An idea of his activity may be conveyed by the subjects of his letters: G. W. Smalley, John Bright, Thorold Rogers, a coöperative congress ; the working people of England ; Thomas Hughes, W. H. Channing, meeting for free Christian Union, Athanase Coquerel, J. J. Taylor, James Martineau ; Scientific Interviews, Professor Tyndall, Philosophical Club, Professor Huxley ; Mr. Congreve and Positivism, Dr. Carpenter ; Herbert Spencer ; Thomas Carlyle ; Louis Blanc ; Frances Power Cobbe ; Henry Morley ; English railways, porters, cabmen, horses ; English hotels, costume, business habits, mode of speaking, etc. These manifold themes are treated deliberately, carefully, always discerningly, usually with all needed fullness. In cases where his sympathy was enlisted, or where the public interest might be supposed to be secure, the notice became discussion, intelligent and ample.

The early summer was spent in travel, of which no record remains. For him there would not be much in Paris, or any smaller cities between London and the delightful valley where lies the charming Baden-Baden, the favorite summer resort of his wife's family. Here the tired man had rest. Early in August he started for a few weeks' travel in Switzerland and Southern Germany. His course led directly to Geneva by way of Basle and Neuchâtel; thence to Chamouny, Martigny, Villeneuve, Vevey, Berne, Interlaken, and over the Brunig to Lucerne, stopping on the road long enough to visit places of interest, enjoy the scenery, and take in the spirit of the country; from Lucerne to Fluelen, up the St. Gothard and Furca Passes to the Rhone glacier, coming back to Lucerne. This was a fresh starting-point to Zürich, Schaffhausen, Constance, and Germany. Ulm, Augsburg, Nuremberg, Hof, and Dresden led by slow stages to Berlin, which was reached in season for the Humboldt festival, September 14th. Here were Mr. and Mrs. George Bancroft, and here a delightful week was spent in public and private festivities. From Berlin the travelers went to Hamburg for a few days, thence back to Stuttgart through

Hanover, Frankfort, Mannheim, and Heidelberg. At Stuttgart there was another rest from September 26th to October 26th.

From Stuttgart Mr. Ripley and his wife went to Munich, Vienna, over the Semmering Pass to Gratz, Trieste, Venice, Milan, Bologna, Florence, to Rome. Neither Munich nor Vienna engaged long or deeply a man who had no passionate love for painting, sculpture, music, or the purely æsthetic arts which minister so largely to the enjoyment of strangers in those pleasant cities. The grandeur of the Semmering Pass impressed him as much by the comfort of its railway accommodations and the skill of the engineering as by the wildness of its wintry landscape. The charming town of Gratz was interesting through the refinement of its society, the intellectual character of its best people, and the beauty of its situation. At Trieste he visited the tomb of Winkelmann, and renewed his old acquaintance with Mr. A. W. Thayer, the devotee of Beethoven. Venice detained him a few days, but had no enchantment for him. In Milan he admired the cleanly streets and well-developed population. The art of Florence engaged him less than the schools, churches, sanitary condition, and municipal regulations of the town. The Florence of the future was more interesting to him than the

Florence of the past. Between Florence and
Rome he made no stop, though Perugia and
Assisi both lay in his track. His impressions
of Rome are best conveyed in the letters which
he sent to "The Tribune," wherein he described
not only the Œcumenical Council which he
went there to portray, but the city itself, as it
appeared twelve years ago. On the whole, it is
not probable that the famous gathering in the
Eternal City had any more capable critic than
he. Scholars inside the Church were prejudiced one way; scholars outside the Church
were prejudiced another. Mr. Ripley was a
Protestant, but he was a philosopher and a man
of letters, serious as well as candid, as free
from prejudices as one can be who has convictions; for thoughtfulness and love of truth
combined to make him just. He was a close
observer of whatsoever came under his eye; for
example, in Rome he noticed that the horses
were shod only on the forefeet, and were driven
with a nose-band instead of a bit, in single
harness, though provided with a safety rein
communicating with a curb-bit in case of need.
He descants on the health of Rome, and makes
shrewd observations on the evil mode of building, ventilation, heating. A little hump-backed
beggar girl on the Spanish steps attracts his
attention and enlists his interest more than the

grandees. The Jews in the Ghetto engage his
sympathy by their family affection, their industry, their sobriety, and their patience. He
is disappointed in the beauty of feature and
form of the Roman women. He studies the
countenances of the priests, the habits of the
common people, the effects of the Catholic religion and the papal rule on the population,
the organization of instruction, the character of
journalism, and whatever besides may concern
an observer of society.

As the proceedings of the Council became
monotonous and spring advanced, Mr. and Mrs.
Ripley left Rome for a short trip to the south
of Italy, Naples, Palermo, of which no record
remains. The climate was not favorable to excursions, and, under such circumstances, there is
little enjoyment in those regions, especially to
a traveler who is without home pursuits. The
summer brought them back to Germany and
to the routine of family life, always so grateful
to this man of studious habits. His hearty enjoyment of intellectual things and of New England associations was amusingly shown in the
delight he expressed on discovering at a book-
shop a volume of Mr. Emerson's essays, which
had appeared since his departure from home.
His glee finds voice in his journal, where it is
unusual that so much space is given to any one
subject : —

I discovered a copy of Emerson's "Society and Solitude," republished in London by Sampson Low. The sight of it was like manna in the wilderness. I became the happy owner of it at once, and it afforded me a rich feast for the rest of the journey. Some portions of it, I think, are equal to anything that Emerson has ever written. Emerson is a great master in his way. His style has an incomparable charm. Its silvery rhythm captivates the ear. The affluence of his illustrations diffuses a flavor of oriental spicery over his pages. As he confesses in the essay on "Books," his learning is second-hand; but everything sticks which his mind can appropriate. He defends the use of translations, and I doubt whether he has ever read ten pages of his great authorities, Plato, Plutarch, Montaigne, or Goethe, in the original. He is certainly no friend of profound study, any more than of philosophical speculation. Give him a few brilliant and suggestive glimpses, and he is content. His catalogue of books is limited in the extreme, and presents few hints of practical value. Much of the work is devoted to the comparative influence of solitude and society, in addition to the chapter with that title. The subject is touched in several of the essays, especially in those on "Clubs" and "Domestic Life." Emerson is fond of conversation, but it always disappoints him. With him it is an experiment constantly repeated, but always without success. His final conclusion is that the true man has no companion. There may be times when two persons may hold genuine communion, but the presence of a third person is impertinent, and always breaks the charm. Such occasions, however, are rare, and must be numbered by moments, and not by hours. His remarks on Art show his want of philosophic culture. The principal point which he urges is that Nature is the foundation of Art, and that the great Artist is spontaneous, and not reflective; both good points, but by no means original. Take away the splendid language in which they are clothed, I find that but little valuable instruction remains. There are frequent hints of the grand Platonic theory of the True, the Beautiful, the Good, as the exponents of the Infinite in Humanity, which long since ripened in my mind, as the true " Intellectual System of the Universe ; " but he does not appear to be aware of its fathomless significance.

In thus renewing my acquaintance with Emerson, I am struck with certain rare combinations which may serve to explain his position. His rejection of dogmas is cool and merciless; but he shows no sympathy with vulgar and destructive radicalism. He asserts an unlimited freedom of the individual, but maintains moral tone, rigid almost to asceticism. With the wild havoc which he makes of popular opinion, he always respects the dignity of human nature. Emerson is essentially a poet. His intuitions are in the form of images. Few men have such positive tendencies toward the Ideal. But his sympathy with external nature is equally strong. He is a keen and accurate observer. His perceptions are true, so far as concerns the material world and the qualities of character that are universal in man. His judgment of individuals is often prejudiced. The practical shrewdness interwoven with his poetical nature is one of the secrets of his power. You attempt to follow his lofty flight among the purple clouds, almost believing that he has "hitched his wagon to a star," when he suddenly drops down to earth, and surprises you with an utterance of the homeliest wisdom. On this account, when they get over the novelty of his manner, plain men are apt to find themselves at home with him. His acquaintance with common things, all household ways and words, the processes of every-day life on the farm, in the kitchen and stable, as well as in the drawing-room and library, engages their attention, and produces a certain kindly warmth of fellowship, which would seem to be incompatible with the coldness of his nature. Emerson is not without a tincture of science. He often makes a happy use of its results, in the way of comparison and illustration. But I do not suppose that he could follow a demonstration of Euclid, or one of the fine analyses in physics of Tyndall or Huxley. Of such a writer as Herbert Spencer he has probably no more than a faint comprehension. Emerson has less wit than I have usually been inclined to believe ; of humor only a slender trace. Perhaps the subtlety and refinement of his illustrations may sometimes have the appearance of wit, but not its real flavor or effect.

It may be interesting to compare this with an earlier sketch : —

With the admiration that Mr. Emerson's works

have called forth to so remarkable an extent, it would be a poor compliment to the understanding of his readers to question their extraordinary merit. There must be something in their intrinsic character which touches a deep chord in the human heart, for they are almost entirely destitute of the qualities which are usually the conditions of a high reputation.

One is immediately struck with the passionless tone in which Mr. Emerson's statements are set forth. They seem like the utterance of a being who has no part in flesh and blood. He is never beguiled into error by the indulgence of his sympathies. His words are dealt out with an elaborate nicety, as if they were the dread oracles of fate. This habitual reticence gives a peculiar coloring to his style. It has the purity, the radiant whiteness, of the virgin snow, but also its coldness. . . .

The passionless tone of his writings, combined with the tendency to a sharp and unrelenting analysis, preserves Mr. Emerson from every symptom of a sectarian or party bias. . . . In fact, his aversion to system would prevent him, under any circumstances, from exerting a more than individual influence; system to him is slavery. . . . If we may guess the methods naturally adopted by his intellect, from the universal character of his writings, we should say that any regular sequence or continuity of thought was altogether foreign to his habits. He lives in the sphere of contemplation, not of consecutive reflection. We find no traces of the progressive evolution of thought which produces such an admirable effect in works, for instance, like the Dialogues of Plato, which Mr. Emerson cannot but acknowledge as masterpieces of human genius. . . .

Nor in the sphere of moral convictions is Mr. Emerson free from similar inconsequences. He pays a profound homage to the moral sentiment in man, the eternal law of right, which manifests itself equally in purity of heart and the gravitation of the planets, but he has no perception of the passionate humanity, the potent attraction, which identifies private and universal interests; and accordingly he finds the highest form of character in the preservation of a stern, frigid, stoical individuality. This error is the cardinal defect of his writings, and exhausts them of the moral vitality and vigor which would give an electric glow to his brilliant intuitions. . . .

The secret of Mr. Emerson's unquestionable strength lies in the profound sincerity of his nature. In his freedom from all affectation, in his attachment to reality, in his indignant rejection of all varnish, gilding, and foppery, whether in character or in literature, he has scarcely an equal. He looks at the universe with his own eyes, and presents the report of his vision, like the testimony of a man under oath. He feels the intrinsic baseness of deception, and is equally unwilling to play the part of a pretender or a dupe. In listening even to his mystic suggestions, you are sure that no attempt is made to put you off with words, and that the obscurest expression stands for some fact in the mind of the speaker. He gives you himself, and not the dry bones of some grisly ancestor.

This truthfulness to himself is the pledge of originality. His writings thus possess the sparkling freshness of a salient fountain. His thought and his imgery alike are the product of his own nature. They could not have been derived from any other source. Used by any one but himself, they would appear forced and trivial. But flowing in their honeyed sweetness from his lips, they seem so redolent of all delicious aromas that they might even allure the swarm of bees that rested on the mouth of Plato.

Mr. Emerson's instincts impel him to penetrate to the hidden essence of things. He is never content with the most obvious view, which is often only the mask of reality. If this sometimes gives his pages an air of too subtle refinement, and leads us to suspect that many of his Orphic sentences are only ingenious conceits or brilliant paradoxes, it also adds a marvelous force to the frequently occurring passages which startle us by the radiant light they throw on subjects which had been concealed in the "Infinite Profound." This tendency characterizes all his judgments of man, of history, and of literature. His opinions derive a peculiar value from their unceasing exercise. Even when we are compelled to show them no quarter, it is never on the ground of their being superficial or commonplace.

His philosophy, which teaches that God and himself are the sole existences, is confirmed by his personal idiosyncrasies. Hence he leaves no realm of beauty unvisited. He gathers the most impressive and magnificent images from every sphere of nature, from the loftiest to the lowest. The plow in the fur row, "the meal in the tub, and the milk in the pan," present him no less fruitful sources of inspiration than the starry heavens and the purple dawn. Coldly as he looks on individual life and sympathy in themselves considered, he loves to draw materials for his affluent poetical eloquence from the humblest phases of humanity. He has sufficient familiarity with the lore of books to furnish out a dozen pedants. In the exuberant life of his expressions we never think of his learning, because he has not been mastered by it himself.

But charming as all this was, the worker could not remain idle. A socialist convention at Stuttgart excited an ardent interest in the old Brook Farmer, whose aspirations after a better human condition never became cool, and who, though very far from being a socialist in any customary sense, could not help watching sympathetically any movements looking towards a readjustment of social relations. This, too, was the summer of the war between France and Prussia, the beginnings and early stages of which he reported in four remarkable letters.

In the autumn of 1870 he was again in New York, at his post of duty, rejoicing in the exercise of his literary faculties under conditions of his own choosing, and in New York he passed the remainder of his days.

CHAPTER VIII.

RECOGNITION.

A NATIONAL INSTITUTE of Letters, Arts, and Sciences was projected in 1868, in the organization of which Mr. Ripley took an active part, and in the conduct of which he would have been prominent, if it had succeeded. The plan commanded his entire sympathy. So hearty was his interest that he spoke of his membership in a slight sketch of himself, made for a biographical volume, and, in his journal, soliloquized in a strain of earnestness that is interesting in itself, but especially interesting as revealing the bent of his disposition : —

For myself, I have no ambition to be gratified in the matter. I rather like the consciousness of possessing merit, which, with my want of sympathy with the present form of society, I have taken pains to hide, rather than to bring before the public. But it pleases my taste to breathe again the intellectual and literary atmosphere in which I was so much at home in Boston, — to which I am so much a stranger in New York. Hence, this Institute awakens in me an nterest something like those glorious reunions of old

18

times. The presence of great, or even greatly culti vated, men exerts a certain gracious magnetism over my nature, calls out my best faculties, and gives me a higher consciousness.

But, above all, this Institute may do much toward spreading sound knowledge, elevating the intellectual standard, and giving a healthy tone to literature in this country. I feel something as Buckminster did when he said that he was justified in laying out so much money on the purchase of books, because his library might have some effect in preventing the country from lapsing into "unlettered barbarism," to which it was exposed by the power of the money-making interest.

Hence, I mean to work for the Institute as far as I can, without neglecting other duties. It will give me a stronger tie to society; it will help to brighten and keep fresh my powers; it will open to me a sphere for the use of gifts that have lain dormant for some time, and enable me to do more for the objects to which my life has been devoted, the improvement and elevation of mankind.

In February, 1874, the choice fell on him to deliver the address on occasion of laying the corner-stone of the new Tribune building on the site of the old one. His words are worth remembering : —

FRIENDS AND FELLOW-LABORERS, — We have assembled to-day in commemoration of the past and for the consecration of the future. The origina.

foundation of " The Tribune" was laid in sentiment
and ideas. Horace Greeley was a man of no less profound convictions than of lofty aspirations. The ten-
derness of his emotional nature was matched by the
strength of his intellect. He was a believer in the
progress of thought and the development of science;
in the progress of society and the development of
humanity. Under the influence of this inspiration,
" The Tribune" was established more than thirty
years ago. At that time its basis was spiritual, and
not material; strong in ideas, but not powerful in
brick and mortar, in granite or marble, in machinery
or in money. We have come to-day not to remove
this foundation, but to combine it with other elements,
and thus to give it renewed strength and consistency.
It is our purpose to clothe the spiritual germ with a
material body, to incorporate the invisible forces
which inspired the heart of our founder in a visible
form, in the shape of a goodly temple, massive in its
foundation, fair in its proportions, and sound in its
purposes. The new "Tribune" of to-day, like the
old "Tribune" of the past, is to be consecrated to the
development of ideas, the exposition of principles, and
the promulgation of truth. The ceremony which is
now about to be performed typifies the union of spiritual agencies with material conditions, and thus possesses a significance and beauty which anticipate the
character of the coming age. The future which lies
before us, it is perhaps not presumptuous to affirm,
will be marked by a magnificent synthesis of the
orces of material nature and the power of spiritual
deas.

Allow me one word in illustration of this prophecy and I will yield the place to the fair hands and the fair spirit whose presence on this occasion crowns the scene with a tender grace.

About two years before the establishment of "The Tribune," dating from the death of Hegel in 1831, and of Goethe in the following year, the tendency of thought on the continent of Europe, which had been of an intensely ideal or spiritual character, began to assume an opposite direction. Physical researches rapidly took precedence of metaphysical speculation. Positive science was inaugurated in the place of abstract philosophy. The spiritual order was well-nigh eclipsed by the wonderful achievements of the material order. A new dynasty arose which knew not Joseph, and the ancient names of Plato and Descartes and Leibnitz were dethroned by the stalwart host which took possession of the domain of physical science. I need not rehearse the splendid discoveries which have signalized this period. Such acquisitions to the treasury of positive human knowledge have never been made in an equal time in the history of thought. More light has been thrown on the material conditions of our existence on earth than has been enjoyed before, since the morning-stars first sang together. But the signs of the times indicate the commencement of a reaction. The age accepts the results of physical research, but refuses to regard them as the limit of rational belief. In resolving matter into molecules and molecules into atoms, the most illustrious cultivators of physical science cheerfully confess tha they arrive at invisible forces, which no crucible can analyze, no microscope detect, no arithmetic explain. The alleged materialism of Tyndall and Huxley thus affords an unexpected support to the idealism of Berkeley.

" The Tribune," it may be predicted, will continue to represent the intellectual spirit of the age. Faithful to its past history, it will welcome every new discovery of truth. Free from the limitations of party, in philosophy or religion, in politics or science, it will embrace a wider range of thought, and pursue a higher aim in the interests of humanity. Watching with its hundred eyes the events of the passing time, it will wait for the blush of the morning twilight, which harbingers the dawn of a brighter day. As we now place the votive tablet on its rocky bed, let it symbolize the radiant scroll of human knowledge reposing on the foundation of eternal truth.

That same year (the tribute was richly deserved, for never did private man make his influence more widely or commandingly felt in high places than he) the University of Michigan conferred on him the degree of LL. D. It was fitting that such an honor should be paid by a western college to one who had so closely at heart the welfare of mankind, and who cherished such ardent hopes for the future of humanity. From one of the older institutions of the country, Harvard or Yale, such a tribute might not have been equally appropriate ; for, though advanced in years, he was a child of the new age, not a creature of the past so much as a builder of the coming civilization. From this moment he was a Doctor of Laws, — he, the disciple of a spiritual philosophy, the inaugurator of Brook Farm, the prophet of a better dispensation, the critic of codes and institutions, the devotee of ideas, the less than half-hearted observer of forms which failed to convey a thought. That the honor was welcome we may easily believe, for the recognition of merit is always gratifying to its possessor; and probably it was not the less welcome as coming from the land of promise.

No one took more hearty interest than he in the tributes of respect that were paid to his friend Bayard Taylor after his appointment as Minister to Berlin, and previous to his departure on his mission. The Penn Club of Philadelphia invited him to a reception, which he could not attend, but to which he sent a response full of admiration for the traveler, journalist, poet, and man of letters, who had gladdened every State in the Union, and who, without doubt, would apply the old Quaker virtues to his new sphere as a diplomatist. The condition of his health also forbade his taking part at the banquet given to Mr. Taylor in New York. At the final hour he was obliged to send the following note : —

37 WEST 19TH STREET, *April* 4, 1878.

DEAR MR. COWDIN, — At the last moment I find,
as I feared, that my health will not permit me to attend the banquet this evening.

Having labored side by side with Bayard Taylor
for so many years, — for, strange as it may appear, to-
night he is my senior in the profession of journalism
in this city, — having so long witnessed his devotion
to duty, his energy of action, the kindliness of his disposition, and the sweet and humane piety of his nature, if I may so call it, as manifested in the love of
whatever is beautiful and good, I should have been
gratified to comply with your request to "offer a few
remarks;" but as I cannot now expand into a speech,
I will ask your leave to offer a sentiment: —

"Our honored and beloved guest: the pupil of two
school-masters of the most widely opposite character,
— the immortal founder of Pennsylvania and the
illustrious poet of Germany, — who, combining the
home-bred principles of William Penn with the cult-
ured wisdom of Goethe, will bring the power of simplicity to the practice of diplomacy.

> Whose armor is his honest thought,
> And simple truth his utmost skill. "

I remain, dear Mr Cowdin, yours faithfully,

GEO. RIPLEY.

His feeling in regard to William Cullen Bry
ant, who died in June of the same year, is expressed in the draft of an epitaph, which was
found among his papers. It was never used : --

Sacred to the Memory of
W. C. B.
In order of time and excellence of genius
one of the fathers of American poetry;
a writer of consummate English prose; by his wisdom
and insight a journalist of masterly power;
though holding no public office,
statesman, of incorruptible integrity, of lofty pa-
triotism, and of supreme devotion to the highest
interests of his country.
As a man, austere, religious, self-contained;
his life was an expression of his poetry,
his death an illustration of the spirit of " Thanatopsis."
B. Nov. 3, 1794.

When Oliver Wendell Holmes reached his
seventieth birthday nothing was more natural
than that the publishers of " The Atlantic
Monthly," which he had glorified by his genius,
should celebrate the occasion by a banquet; nor
was anything more natural than their wish that
the literary editor of " The Tribune " should
grace it by his presence. He could not go to
Boston, but he responded to the invitation in a
tone that gave assurance of his sincere affection
for the guest, and of his readiness to acknowledge the service of all good workers in the cause
of letters. The word of regret which represented
him at the Brunswick breakfast carried in it a
heart full of thanks: —

New York, *November* 25, 1879.

DEAR SIR, — I am truly sorry that it is not in my power to accept your kind invitation. It would give me the sincerest pleasure to join in the honors to the beloved poet, who, from my pupil in the university, has become my teacher in the high school of life. I would fain add a leaf to the laurel which will crown his brow, and confess my debt for the smiling wisdom, the exquisite humor, the joyous hilarity, the tender pathos that softens the lambent wit of the man who, on the verge of old age, has never grown old, and with the experience of years preserves the freshness of youth.

With my best wishes that the light of his eventide may long shine with the morning beauty of his early manhood, I am most cordially,

His friend and yours, GEO. RIPLEY.

When the plan of a "Memorial History of Boston" was outlined, a chapter entitled "Boston's Place in the History of Philosophic Thought," in the fourth and last volume, was, naturally, assigned to Mr. J. Elliot Cabot, a Boston man, living near Boston, an accomplished scholar, a diligent student in philosophy, a profound and original thinker on the problems which have most deeply engaged the human mind. On his declining the task by reason of preoccupation, it was, at the suggestion of excellent judges, Dr. F. H. Hedge being of the number, offered to Mr. Ripley, as the best man they could have; his remoteness from Boston being waived in consideration of the impartiality and comprehensiveness which distance might give to his view. He, though immersed in literary occupation, accepted the duty at once, and instantly set about the studies preparatory to his sketch. He measured his space, selected his names, refreshed and fortified his recollections, searched the processes of development, wrote, rewrote, weighed his words in scales of exact justice, and submitted his manuscript to his intimate friend George Bancroft before trusting it to the publisher. The pen dropped from his fingers midway in the work, and the uncompleted chapter was finished by another hand; admirably finished, too, but not quite according to the plan which Mr. Ripley laid out, and which he alone could complete. The scheme was as remarkable for clearness as it was for candor of judgment, and the composition is among the most careful productions of his skill. The space accorded to the writer did not permit a more extended range of thought, it is simply astonishing that, having no more room, so much that was valuable should have been compressed into it. It is matter of regret that Mr. Ripley's excessive modesty prevented his yielding to Dr. Channing's frequent request that he would write an account of mod ern philosophical systems. The fragment left us in the "Memorial History" — so penetrating, calm, and fair — makes the regret keen. A comprehensive work done in that spirit would possess singular worth; for such complete exclusion of the partisan temper, combined with firmness of intellectual description, rare in any discussion, is quite unexampled in the discussion of those tormenting subjects which have been closely bound up with the issues of religious faith. The admixture of sentimentality with charitableness commonly weakens the toleration, and makes the impartiality to be something less than justice. In the case of George Ripley the line between religious feeling and philosophic thought was so sharply drawn that he could be at the same time discerning and believing, devout and fair. In his disposition, literature and dogma never clashed. The intellectual poise was perfect. However, at times, the strength of his personal affections might incline him to overpraise the work of a friend, a sense of equity, stealing out in some critical line or phrase, was certain to render the verdict true on the whole.

The honors which bore witness to the appreciation of George Ripley's extraordinary capacity, the general recognition of his literary merit, the high place assigned to him as a critic of books, the public and private admission of his authority in the realm of letters, did not in the least degree impair his conscientiousness, or diminish the carefulness of his work. No obscure man toiling for fame labored harder than he did to meet every condition of excellence. His patience was inexhaustible; his persistency was prodigious. He would sit in his chair all day long, reading and writing, unconscious of fatigue, insensible to annoyance, heedless even of interruption, never complaining of over-pressure, piercing the heart of a volume with a glance, and throwing off page after page of manuscript with an ease of touch which betokened the trained mind as well as the practiced hand. To report the literary achievement of the last ten years of his life would be impossible. The columns of " The Tribune " bear witness to an amazing variety of toil, all executed with fidelity, much of it with distinguished power, some of it with rare elegance and grace of execution. The range of topics embraces the extremes of mental productiveness from the speculations of philosophy to creations of fancy. Within this period come the remarkable papers on Voltaire, Rousseau, Goethe, Carlyle, Bryant, which at the time they appeared were thought marvels of literary performance. Some of his most acute judgments of opinions and men are found in these fugitive notices; some of his most penetrating glances into the unrevealed tendencies of thought. The review of Bascom's "Comparative Psychology" is a luminous essay on the distinctions of thought which separate the schools of mental science from each other; the review of Arnold's "Literature and Dogma" is a good example of the resolution with which the truth is insisted on, in spite of the literary grace that conceals and the ingenious speculation that confuses it. In no instance is judgment perverted. His antipathy to Joaquin Miller (to cite a strong example) does not prevent him from giving Miller credit for "boldness of conception, vividness of description, and freshness and force of utterance."

The characteristics of Mr. Ripley's literary method may easily be described. The feature of his work which stands out conspicuously is faithfulness of conception and execution. Before dealing with any matter of importance he made careful preparation. Among his papers are sketches and studies for his review of Professor Bascom's book, for example. A vast deal of thought was bestowed on the chapter in the "Memorial History of Boston;" many scraps of paper, containing hints, suggestions, names of prominent thinkers, titles of books, which formed links in the chain of philosophical development. In mastering the system of Hartmann, nothing would do but a study of the author in the original German. The review of Professor Bowen's volume had beneath it a close personal acquaintance with the systems there described. The estimates of Voltaire, Rousseau, Lessing, Goethe, Huxley, Spencer, to mention no more, were the result of wide reading, patient thought, and large consideration of historic mental conditions. His shortest notices usually contain some intimation of knowledge acquired in independent investigations. A distinguished orator, being asked how he avoided in public the use of slang phrases, replied, " By always avoiding the use of them in private intercourse." On no easier terms can purity of speech be preserved.

The competency of Mr. Ripley's literary judgments has often been remarked on. He did not wait till others had spoken, and then venture an opinion. He spoke at once, and he spoke with confidence, as one who had good reason for what he said. Whether the book in question was the " Scarlet Letter," the " Origin of Species," or the " Light of Asia," the verdict was equally prompt and decided. There was no dogmatism, no boasting, no claim to special insight, no affectation of patronage ; simply a quiet recognition of talent and an appreciation of its value in the world of letters. That his judgments were generally confirmed by specialists is an evidence of their intrinsic worth; that they were usually ratified by the public testifies to his knowledge of the public taste.

The literary unprejudiced spirit of his criticisms appears in his treatment, so generous, yet so nicely balanced, of such totally dissimilar men as George H. Lewes and Herbert Spencer, the former of whom he distrusted, while in the latter he had confidence. The criticism on Judge Tourgee's novel, "A Fool's Errand," is a remarkable instance of equitable judgment on the part of one whose anti-slavery feelings were not ardent, and whose political sympathies, though clear, were not tinctured by party fanaticism. His agreement or disagreement with the author under review was felt to have no connection with the verdict of the critic.

It has been said again and again, in fact it has become the fashion to say, that George Ripley belonged to the class of "genial" critics, who prophesy smooth things, who seldom notice what they cannot praise, who pick out of books the passages they can commend, and encourage where they should condemn. They who say this cannot be thinking of the frequent instances in which he exposed literary preten sion, or of the severity of his treatment when ever shallowness or charlatanism tried to get access to the public ear. A survey of his work during a period of thirty years leaves no impression of such literary "good-nature" as he has been charged with. The careful reader will not fail to notice the qualification which is introduced into his most eulogistic articles, sometimes in a paragraph, sometimes in a line, sometimes in a guarded expression. Even his friends, who could not doubt his private affection, have occasionally been surprised at the chariness of his admiration for their most excellent performance ; supposing that he would share their enthusiastic sentiments towards their achievement, or that, if he lacked the discernment, he would, at all events, be restrained by personal attachment from making the newspaper a confidant of his indifference.

For the rest, his appreciation of excellence, his desire to encourage excellence wherever found, his sense of the importance of calling forth the intellectual stores of the people, his confidence in the medicinal qualities of praise, his sympathy with struggling talent, his natural hopefulness, and his steady allowance for imperfection in all human workmanship abundantly explain the so-called "geniality" of his literary temper. He was afraid of chilling the buds of genius. He believed in sunshine, in warm persuasive, enticing air, in gentle breezes, in gracious showers of rain, in balmy seasons; well knowing how easily ambition is disheartened. Many an author whose place in the world of letters is secure looks back gratefully to his helping counsel, ascribing to him the strong impulse which was needed to overcome the diffidence of youth; and many an author, whose diffidence required pruning in order that the fine fruit of talent might appear, is grateful to him for kind suggestion thrown in at the decisive moment. Both praise and blame were felt to be judicious as well as benignant. The judiciousness tempered the benignity; but the benignity furnished the motive for the judiciousness.

His modesty was as remarkable as his capacity. A young friend, ambitious and industrious, having in the dedication of his first book spoken of him as " the Nestor of ' The Tribune,' " and called him " the Father of Literary Criticism in the American Press," received from him the following note : —

OFFICE OF THE AMERICAN CYCLOPÆDIA,
NEW YORK, *May* 20, 1875.

MY DEAR W——, — I have no objection whatever to your connecting my name with yours in your forthcoming volume, if it will be any pleasure to you or any service to your book; on the contrary, your

19

friendly recognition is very agreeable to me. But I must unequivocally, decidedly, peremptorily — and if there is any other longer and stronger dictionary word, please pick it out — protest against the extravagant and untenable form in which you have worded it. Though an old soldier, I am no Nestor; though of the masculine gender, no father of American literary criticism, nor of anything, or anybody else. When I have the pleasure of seeing you again, I will enlighten your youthful mind on the history of American criticism, and you will hide your head in remorse. At present think of Bryant, Verplanck, Cogswell, Henry, Godwin, Greeley, Raymond, in New York; Dana, Channing, Tudor, Willard, Sparks, Everett, Palfrey, Willard Phillips, in Boston, — all of whom were distinguished reviewers and critics before my name was ever heard of, except as "a Socinian minister, who left his pulpit in order to reform the world by cultivating onions" (Carlyle).

As I have corrected and curtailed the inscription, it is modest and inoffensive, and " if it does no good will not do any harm."

If you have any account of conversations with the present victim, I should be glad to see the report, and meantime, my good old trapper,

I am yours ever,   G. R.

It is unnecessary to say that the inscription was not printed as designed, and yet it was true in the main. George Ripley was the " father of literary criticism in the American press," though not, of course, in America. The American press was not fairly in existence in the time of Sparks, Everett, Palfrey, and others named in the above letter. There were local papers, of wider or narrower influence, and they contained, incidentally, valuable literary criticism. But the empire of a few great journals — an empire built upon the basis of cheap postage, and made possible by the accumulation of talent and the expenditure of money — was established later. " The Tribune" is barely forty years old; and, previous to its birth, criticism of the higher order was confined to magazines like " The North American Review" (quarterly), " The Christian Examiner" (bi-monthly), " The Literary Messenger," Arthur's " Home Gazette," and two or three others of limited circulation. The work of Mr. Ripley was naturally less ponderously elaborate than the heavier periodicals required; it was a combination of the scholarly and the popular as yet unattempted: precisely there lay its originality, and original in a very true sense it undoubtedly was. Others — Bryant, Raymond, Greeley — did admirable service by the way, but the greater portion of their strength was devoted to political discussion. George Ripley gave all his time and all his energy to literary criticism, spending on it, too, the full resources of a richly furnished mind, and infusing into it the spirit of a broad and noble training.

His intellectual temperament aided him in his task. The absence of passion was a great advantage. The lack of ardent partisan feeling made possible the calm, clear, judicial temper so necessary to the critic. The want of what may be called the " artistic constitution," which delights in music, painting, sculpture, architecture, did something to insure the equability of his poise. His mental force was not wasted by emotion or attenuated by distraction. He was no dreamer, no visionary, no enthusiast, no creature of imagination or fancy. He was, through and through, a critic, gentle but firm, intelligent, exact, holding the interests of truth paramount to all others, always hoping that the interests of truth might be served by the effort of careful writers.

His extreme conscientiousness, amounting to fastidiousness, his jealousy of the movement of his own mind, his absence of personal ambition, his appreciation of intellectual difficulties and individual aberrations, his lack of enjoyment in the creative process, and his habit of austere self-recollection, will help to explain his backwardness in authorship. Not often are author and critic united in the same person. The one art requires different faculties from the other, at all events, a different direction of the facul ties. The author's impulse is outward, away from the centre, towards a waiting, expectant public, desiring to be instructed or entertained. The critic's bent is inward, back to the centre, away from the public, who are not supposed to be interested in his performance. His business is to make distinctions, — to analyze, not to construct, — and in doing this he must come back continually to standards of judgment which exist in his own mind.

That George Ripley was capable of sustaining himself in a long flight was proved by the letters to Andrews Norton, which, together, make a respectable volume, and which might easily have been extended without change of method. The training of Mr. Ripley was in the school of compression. As a preacher, his art consisted in a due proportion of material to space ; in the omission of details and the presentation of results ; in a skillful process of summarizing, length being out of the question, and expansion forbidden by the first conditions of homiletics. As a journalist, he was held to the same rigid rules. The habit of saying all that was necessary in two or three columns compelled him to select salient points, to employ the language of suggestion in preference to the language of description, to bring thoughts to a head, to pass quickly from one matter to another, to dwell on no subject till it became tiresome, and to avoid prolixity as the unpardon-able sin. By the practice of years this habit became imperative. To break through it was all but impossible. At all events, the temptation to break through it lost its charm, and the idea of authorship was put aside. Force of genius might burst the limits of such restrictions ; love of money or of fame might disregard them ; but where genius is quiescent, and the love of money moderate, and the passion for fame cold, the law of repression is imperious, and the mind finds absolute content in the work of reporting the conclusions of more impulsive intellects. How important is the service rendered by minds thus constituted few can appreciate. If faithful to their calling, they may raise the entire level of literary performance ; they will make good work, and only good work, possible ; they will put carelessness to shame. This was the crowning achievement of George Ripley, and this quality in his work was appreciated by fine minds, abroad as well as at home. Professor Tyndall, for instance, through his friend E. L. Youmans, in 1875, sent his " special regards " to Dr. Ripley, saying, " If I publish another edition of the ' Address,' I should almost like to preface it with his article on Martineau. He writes, as he has ever written, with the grasp of a philosopher and the good taste of a gentleman."

CHAPTER IX.

THE END.

GEORGE RIPLEY inherited a robust constitution. His brother Franklin lived to be over seventy. His sister Marianne reached about the same age. George, younger than either, lived longer. His way of life, though laborious, was even, and, with the exception of a few years, calm. His admirable temper threw off the enemies of health, and reduced the perils of mental and moral friction to their smallest dimensions. His habits were simple to the verge of abstemiousness. Without being ascetic in any respect, he had learned how many good things he could do without, and be no worse for the abstinence. His routine of work was regular; he was not disabled by dyspepsia, languor, headache, or heartache; he was not distracted by the vain wish to be somewhere else, or to be otherwise employed. To the wear and tear of toil he was, of course, exposed; but the wear and tear of toil, when unaided by other corroding causes, seldom fret life away. He was a severe worker, not counting hours, or regard-

ing seasons, or taking into account personal
convenience; but as he never neglected the
rules of health, he did not suffer from excessive
application. He enjoyed his sleep and ate his
dinner without fear. In his early life he was
much in the air, took long walks, reveled in
natural influences. At Brook Farm his existence was not allowed to be sedentary. On his
removal to New York the necessity of travers-
ing considerable distances between his residence
and his office supplied the amount of exercise
he required. He never rode when he could
walk. Driving was no recreation to him. His
satisfactions were mental. In his later years
he became portly, though none too much so for
his appearance or comfort, and not at all to the
diminution of his power of work, which continued unabated. He would sit all day at his
table, reading and writing, his industry never
flagging, his spirits never drooping, his judgment never clouded; glad to see the face of a
friend, and overjoyed at the pleasant humor of
his young wife, but contented if left alone,
finding the necessary sources of vitality in his
own healthy nature. His faculties, undisturbed
by the moods which render fitful the activities
of nervous organizations, played with absolute
smoothness, let the weather be what it might
be. A constitutional hilarity preserved him

from despondency, and so long as his health remained essentially unimpaired his intellectual activity went on with the evenness of mechanism.

His eye was fastened on one weak spot. He dreaded taking cold. His influenzas were stubborn and painful. He often intimated that the source of danger was in his chest, and his knowledge of physiology kept that danger ever before him. Possibly, his precautions were excessive. During the last winter preceding his decease he did not leave the house, but sat from morning till night at his desk, without exercise, or the bracing tonic of the outer air. The world came to him in the persons of friends and in the breezy presence of his wife, who kept him informed of the goings-on of the social world. For years it had been his custom to absent himself from the Tribune Office, and to save time by having books sent to him, thus increasing his sedentary habit. Still his health did not suffer apparently from the confinement, though occasionally a premonitory symptom kept him in mind of his infirmity. In the winter of 1879–80 painful symptoms alarmed him; but it was not till the spring was far advanced that the final attack was made. No care or skill availed then to beat it off. It soon became evident that he must succumb to the enemy. The

last " opinion " sent to the Harpers bears the
date June 21, 1880, — the subject was a book
entitled " The Fierce Spirit of Liberty," — and
the latter half of it was written by Mrs. Ripley.
The last printed review, that of Horace Bushnell's Biography, bears date June 18th. That
this work was done with painful effort is probable from the circumstance that the last article
preserved in the scrap-book, where, as a rule,
his papers were kept, was printed June 5th.
It is singular that the subject of the notice was
a volume called " New England Bygones."
The genial spirit of the man enjoyed the theme,
for he himself was of New England stock ; the
New England temper animated him ; even the
New England dishes suited his palate ; his
memory loved to haunt the scenes of Thanksgiving ; he was proud of the New England traditions ; something of New England austerity
clung to his morals ; the New England " enthusiasm for humanity " was part of his constitution ; his religion preserved the New England
sobriety and earnestness, though the theological
intensity was lost. He could feel when he
could no longer perceive. The grace of resignation was born in him, and when the time came
that he must stop doing and practice patience
he was ready.

His final illness was protracted and painful.

An incessant restlessness possessed him; distress for breath rendered night and day miserable. No medical skill, no loving devotion, gave relief. In the moments when suffering permitted he was fully himself; affectionate, loyal to the best faith of his earlier time, glad to see his friends, more than glad to see those who revived in him the recollection of his heroic days. The nature of his disease forbade his saying much; but what he did say out of a clear mind was quite worthy of himself. After he abandoned the religious beliefs of his youth he never returned to them, never deplored their absence, though a copy of the hymns of Dr. Watts lay on his study table for use. He loved life, but had no dread of death. He feared pain, but knew how to bear it. He clung to his friends, and his friends did not forsake him. He depended on the care of his wife, and it was lavished on him to the last. In his closing hours he called for no other support from without. He died on the 4th of July, 1880. The news of his death reached many before the news of his sickness, for his daily existence had long been uneventful, and only those nearest to him were at all aware of his condition. The distress incidental to a recumbent position made his bed unwelcome. Even when mortally ill he preferred a sitting posture; and this conveyed an idea that he was stronger than he really was. He died in his writing-room, in his chair, — at his post of duty to the very end.

Though his position in the world of literature had long been acknowledged, his decease brought it freshly to men's minds. From one end of the country to the other the tributes to his enlightened capacity, to his distinguished knowledge, to his eminent skill as a discerner of thoughts, came in. Editors, writers of every class, critics of diverse schools, confessed his power, and celebrated the service he had rendered to American literature. There was no dissentient voice. His was felt to be a general loss. In the absence of his own pastor (the son of a cordial friend of his youth) a comparative stranger spoke the last words at his funeral, making amends for lack of intimacy by warmth of expression ; thus doing justice to one aspect of him which was little understood, the hearty human sympathy there was in him.

A great concourse of people attended the obsequies. Distinguished men, divines, critics, scholars, editors, architects, scientists, journalists, publicists, men of affairs, artists, were in the assembly. The pall-bearers were the President of Columbia College; the Editor of " Harper's Weekly ; " the representative of the great publishing house he had served so many years an Italian professor and man of letters; the Editor of " The Popular Science Monthly ; " the Editor of " The New York Observer ; " a distinguished college professor ; an eminent German lawyer ; a popular poet ; and the Editor of " The Tribune," whose cordial, faithful friend he had ever been. These nobly represented the many-sided sympathies and universal relations of the man. They were at once personal intimates, professional allies, and intellectual neighbors ; uniting love for the individual with admiration for the writer. If George Bancroft and Parke Godwin had been present, not as distinguished men of letters, but as old comrades, — the former a close temporal and spiritual friend, the latter a brother in the early projects for an associated humanity, — the representation would have been perfect : a Unitarian minister officiating, organized humanity paying its tribute, the broad spirit of modern literature offering its praise, private affection revealing its sense of bereavement. He was buried at Wood-lawn Cemetery, in New York, where a granite monument marks his resting place.

Rev. William Henry Channing, of London, an old comrade and intimate friend of George Ripley, would have prepared for this memoir a full report of his life and a judgment of his character, had pressing engagements permitted.

Circumstances forbade his doing more than write a regretful letter, an extract wherefrom will indicate the spirit in which the tribute would have been offered. It is hardly necessary to add that all who knew well the subject of this biography will render the same testimony to a man they loved as cordially as they admired him.

CAMPDEN HOUSE ROAD, KENSINGTON, LONDON,
Monday, April 7, 1882.

Your disappointment cannot at all equal mine, at my inability to send the promised sketch of our honored compeer, George Ripley. But the ever-widening claims of reform movements, committees, correspondence, etc., etc., have prevented during the whole season; and when, at last, a period of leisure came, my health again broke down, compelling rest.

The more the subject has been thought over, and long-buried memories of our dear friend reappear, the wider and richer the theme opens. And it would need many pages to present the least adequate portraits of George Ripley as a Christian minister, a scholar, an expounder of philosophy, a social reorganizer, a literary critic, an encyclopædist, a friend, and a man. To me, in reviewing his diversified, yet consistent, progressive, and ascending career, he takes a front rank among the many leaders of thought whom it has been my rare privilege to know, in our own republic and in Europe.

Especially would it gratify me to bear my testimony to the generous and quite heroic spirit, whereby he and his great-souled wife were impelled to organize Brook Farm; and to the wise sagacity, genial good-heartedness, friendly sympathy, patience, persistency, and ideal hopefulness with which they energetically helped to carry out that romantic enterprise to the end. They consulted with me from first to last, and opened their confidence as they did to very few; for they knew how warmly and uncompromisingly my conscience, judgment, enthusiastic anticipations of a purer, freer, more beautifully ordered, and deeply religious form of society, responded to their own. For years my reiterated and urgent entreaty was that he should write out his "Record" of that brave experiment, but he constantly refused. And to my last appeal, made during an interview, in the summer of 1880, our final meeting here below, in answer to the question, "*When will* you tell that story, as you alone can tell it?" he replied, with eyes twinkling merrily and his rotund form shaking with laughter, "Whenever I reach my *years of indiscretion!*" And at the close of our prolonged talk he looked at me affectionately, and said, "But for your uncle William's encouragement I never should have undertaken Brook Farm; and but for your unwavering good-cheer I never should have carried on the attempt so long."

It is not claimed that George Ripley was a man of genius, the peer of Irving, Prescott, Motley, Bancroft, Bryant, Emerson, Channing,

or any of the men who have made the age illustrious at home or abroad. It is not claimed
that he was a profound scholar, an original
thinker, even in his favorite department of philosophy, nor yet an accomplished man, in the
usual sense of the word. But it is claimed that
he possessed the literary spirit in a remarkable
degree; that his mind was singularly calm,
even, capacious, and exact; that he was a man
of rare intelligence and master of a pure style
of English. It is claimed that he put his whole
life into the work of interpreting ideas to men,
infusing into letters the earnestness and the
sweetness of character. It is claimed that with
him literature was a high calling, on a line with
the ministry, which he abandoned, or the career
of a reformer, which he undertook at Brook
Farm. One spirit animated all his performance
from beginning to end. The forms of his activity changed; his hope and purpose continued
unfaltering to the last. Whether preaching,
administering, writing, making a Cyclopædia,
or reviewing books, he had one end in view, —
the enlightenment and elevation of mankind.

Southey's fine lines, applied to Sir William
Hamilton in his library, found among George
Ripley's papers, in his own handwriting, partly
express the man : —

My days among the dead are past;
  Around me I behold,
Where'er these casual eyes are cast,
  The mighty minds of old.
My never-failing friends are they
With whom I converse day by day.

My hopes are with the dead; anon
  My place with them will be,
And I with them shall travel on
  Through all futurity;
Yet leaving here a name, I trust,
That will not perish in the dust.

In his old college Commonplace Book, under
date December 5, 1825, he wrote an extract
and comment as follows: "'*A morning* of ardor
and of hope; *a day* of clouds and storms; *an
evening* of gloom closed in by premature darkness: such is the melancholy sum of what the
biography of Men of Letters almost uniformly
presents.' Is this true?"

20

APPENDIX.

—————

THE following letters, which came too late to be inserted in the proper place, are interesting as throwing light on Mr. Ripley's purposes, and as showing how his scheme was regarded by a sympathetic and singularly discerning mind. Mr. Emerson's attitude towards Brook Farm illustrates well his peculiar genius : —

BOSTON, *November* 9, 1840.

MY DEAR SIR, — Our conversation in Concord was of such a general nature, that I do not feel as if you were in complete possession of the idea of the Association which I wish to see established. As we have now a prospect of carrying it into effect, at an early period, I wish to submit the plan more distinctly to your judgment, that you may decide whether it is one that can have the benefit of your aid and coöperation.

Our objects, as you know, are to insure a more natural union between intellectual and manual labor than now exists ; to combine the thinker and the worker, as far as possible, in the same individual ; to guarantee the highest mental freedom, by providing all with labor, adapted to their tastes and talents, and

securing to them the fruits of their industry ; to do
away the necessity of menial services, by opening the
benefits of education and the profits of labor to all ;
and thus to prepare a society of liberal, intelligent,
and cultivated persons, whose relations with each
other would permit a more simple and wholesome
life, than can be led amidst the pressure of our competitive institutions.

To accomplish these objects, we propose to take a
small tract of land, which, under skillful husbandry,
uniting the garden and the farm, will be adequate to
the subsistence of the families ; and to connect with
this a school or college, in which the most complete
instruction shall be given, from the first rudiments to
the highest culture.   Our farm would be a place for
improving the race of men that lived on it ; thought
would preside over the operations of labor, and labor
would contribute to the expansion of thought ; we
should have industry without drudgery, and true
equality without its vulgarity.

An offer has been made to us of a beautiful estate,
on very reasonable terms, on the borders of Newton,
West Roxbury, and Dedham.   I am very familiar
with the premises, having resided on them a part of
last summer, and we might search the country in vain
for anything more eligible.   Our proposal now is for
three or four families to take possession on the first
of April next, to attend to the cultivation of the farm
and the erection of buildings, to prepare for the com-
ng of as many more in the autumn, and thus to commence the institution in the simplest manner, and

with the smallest number, with which it can go into operation at all. It would thus be not less than two or three years, before we should be joined by all who mean to be with us; we should not fall to pieces by our own weight; we should grow up slowly and strong; and the attractiveness of our experiment would win to us all whose society we should want.

The step now to be taken at once is the procuring of funds for the necessary capital. According to the present modification of our plan, a much less sum will be required than that spoken of in our discussions at Concord. We thought then $50,000 would be needed; I find now, after a careful estimate, that $30,000 will purchase the estate and buildings for ten families, and give the required surplus for carrying on the operations for one year.

We propose to raise this sum by a subscription to a joint stock company, among the friends of the institution, the payment of a fixed interest being guaranteed to the subscribers, and the subscription itself secured by the real estate. No man then will be in danger of losing; he will receive as fair an interest as he would from any investment, while at the same time he is contributing towards an institution, in which while the true use of money is retained, its abuses are done away. The sum required cannot come from rich capitalists; their instinct would protest against such an application of their coins; it must be obtained from those who sympathize with our ideas, and who are willing to aid their realization with their money, if not by their personal coöperation. There are some of this description on whom I think we can rely; among ourselves we can produce perhaps $10,000; the remainder must be subscribed for by those who wish us well, whether they mean to unite with us or not.

I can imagine no plan which is suited to carry into effect so many divine ideas as this. If wisely executed, it will be a light over this country and this age. If not the sunrise, it will be the morning star. As a practical man, I see clearly that we must have some such arrangement, or all changes less radical will be nugatory. I believe in the divinity of labor; I wish to "harvest my flesh and blood from the land;" but to do this, I must either be insulated and work to disadvantage, or avail myself of the services of hirelings, who are not of my order, and whom I can scarce make friends; for I must have another to drive the plough, which I hold. I cannot empty a cask of lime upon my grass alone. I wish to see a society of educated friends, working, thinking, and living together, with no strife, except that of each to contribute the most to the benefit of all.

Personally, my tastes and habits would lead me in another direction. I have a passion for being independent of the world, and of every man in it. This I could do easily on the estate which is now offered, and which I could rent at a rate, that with my other resources, would place me in a very agreeable condition, as far as my personal interests were involved. I should have a city of God, on a small scale of my own; and please God, I should hope one day to drive my own cart to market and sell greens. But I feel bound to sacrifice this private feeling, in the hope of a great social good. I shall be anxious to hear from you. Your decision will do much towards settling the question with me, whether the time has come for the fulfillment of a high hope, or whether the work belongs to a future generation. All omens now are favorable; a singular union of diverse talents is ready for the enterprise; everything indicates that we ought to arise and build; and if we let slip this occasion, the unsleeping Nemesis will deprive us of the boon we seek. For myself, I am sure that I can never give so much thought to it again; my mind must act on other objects, and I shall acquiesce in the course of fate, with grief that so fair a light is put out. A small pittance of the wealth which has been thrown away on ignoble objects, during this wild contest for political supremacy, would lay the cornerstone of a house, which would ere long become the desire of nations.

I almost forgot to say that our friends, the " Practical Christians," insist on making their " Standard," — a written document, — a prescribed test. This cuts them off. Perhaps we are better without them. They are good men; they have salt, which we needed with our spice; but we might have proved too liberal, too comprehensive, too much attached to the graces of culture, to suit their ideas. Instead of them, we have the offer of ten or twelve '' Practical Men," from Mr. S. G. May, who himself is deeply interested in the proposal, and would like one day to share in its concerns. Pray write me with as much frankness as I have used towards you, and believe me ever your friend and faithful servant,

GEORGE RIPLEY.

P. S. I ought to add, that in the present stage of the enterprise no proposal is considered as binding. We wish only to know what can probably be relied on, provided always, that no pledge will be accepted until the articles of association are agreed on by all parties.

I recollect you said that if you were sure of com peers of the right stamp you might embark yourself in the adventure : as to this, let me suggest the inquiry, whether our Association should not be composed of various classes of men ? If we have friends whom we love and who love us, I think we should be content to join with others, with whom our personal sympathy is not strong, but whose general ideas coincide with ours, and whose gifts and abilities would make their services important. For instance, I should like to have a good washerwoman in my parish admitted into the plot. She is certainly not a Minerva or a Venus ; but we might educate her two children to wisdom and varied accomplishments, who otherwise will be doomed to drudge through life. The same is true of some farmers and mechanics, whom we should like with us.

BROOK FARM, *December* 17, 1841.

MY DEAR SIR, — I feel so sure of your sympathy in the ideas which our little company are trying to

illustrate, that I do not hèsitate to bespeak your attention to our prospects.

We are now in full operation as a family of workers, teachers, and students ; we feel the deepest inward convictions that for us our mode of life is the
true one, and no attraction would tempt any one of
us to exchange it for that which we have quitted
lately. A rare Providence seems to have smiled on
us in the materials which have been drawn together
on this spot; and so many powers are at work with
us and for us, that I cannot doubt we are destined to
succeed in giving visible expression to some of the
laws of social life, that as yet have been kept in the
background.

We are all of us here full of joy and hope ; we
have overcome great obstacles ; our foundation, I
trust, is wisely laid. We seem to have every element of success, except the hindrances that arise
from our poverty. Some of our friends have put us
in possession of the means of owning the estate we
live on ; and our personal resources are sufficient,
when available, for the immediate improvements we
contemplate. Still, without larger means than are
now at our command, we must labor to great disadvantage, and perhaps retard and seriously injure our
enterprise. Our farming, in a pecuniary view, has
been successful. It has realized ten per cent. net
gain on the value of the estate, which I believe is Mr.
Phinney's mark ; and our income is somewhat more
than our current expenses. But we are called on for
outlays, for absolutely necessary accommodations,

which, though conducted with a Spartan economy, exhaust our available funds, and leave us too restricted for successful operation.

Our resource, in this case, is to request some of those who have faith in us and in our enterprise, not to endow us, or to portion us, but to invest in our stock such sums as they can temporarily part with, and receive therefor a just equivalent. Our shares are $500 each; they are guaranteed five per cent. interest, and may be withdrawn at the pleasure of the subscribers, on giving three months' notice. I have no doubt that an investment would be equally safe, if not equally lucrative, as in any joint-stock company in the Commonwealth, besides essentially aiding in the establishment of an institution, which is believed to contain the seeds of future good to men.

If my confessions should prompt you to seek the ownership of one or more of our shares, I need not say that we should be gratified and greatly forwarded in this the time of our infant struggle and hope ; but if you have any cause to do otherwise, I am sure that you will be no less frank than I have been, and regard this request as if it had never been made.

Your young friend Frank Brown is very well and I hope will do well. Ever yours sincerely,

GEORGE RIPLEY.

Mr. Emerson's reply is without date, and is apparently an unfinished sketch : —

MY DEAR SIR, — It is quite time I made an answer to your proposition that I should venture into your new community. The design appears to me noble and generous, proceeding, as I plainly see, from nothing covert, or selfish, or ambitious, but from a manly and expanding heart and mind. So it makes all men its friends and debtors. It becomes a matter of conscience to entertain it in a friendly spirit, and examine what it has for us.

I have decided not to join it, and yet very slowly and I may almost say with penitence. I am greatly relieved by learning that your coadjutors are now so many that you will no longer attach that importance to the defection of individuals which, you hinted in your letter to me, I or others might possess, — the painful power I mean of preventing the execution of the plan.

My feeling is that the community is not good for me, that it has little to offer me, which, with resolution I cannot procure for myself; that it would not be worth my while to make the difficult exchange of my property in Concord for a share in the new household. I am in many respects placed as I wish to be, in an agreeable neighborhood, in a town which I have some reason to love, and which has respected my freedom so far that I have reason to hope it will in dulge me further when I demand it. I cannot accuse my townsmen or my neighbors of my domestic grievances, only my own sloth and conformity. It seems to me a circuitous and operose way of relieving myself to put upon your community the emancipation which I ought to take on myself. I must assume my own vows.

The institution of domestic hired service is to me very disagreeable. I should like to come one step nearer to nature than this usage permits. But surely I need not sell my house and remove my family to Newton in order to make the experiment of labor and self help. I am already in the act of trying some domestic and social experiments which would gain nothing.

I ought to say that I do not put much trust in any arrangements or combinations, only in the spirit which dictates them. Is that benevolent and divine, they will answer their end. Is there any alloy in that, it will certainly appear in the result.

I have the same answer to make to the proposition of the school. According to my ability and according to your's, you and I do now keep school for all comers, and the energy of our thought and of our will measures our influence.

I do not think I should gain anything, I, who have little skill to converse with people, by a plan of so many parts, and which I comprehend so slowly and bluntly.

I almost shudder to make any statement of my objections to our ways of living, because I see how slowly I shall mend them. My own health and habits of living and those of my wife and my mother are not of that robustness that should give any pledge of enterprise and ability in reform. Nor can I insist with any heat on new methods when I am at work in my study on any literary composition. Yet I think that all I shall solidly do, I must do alone, and

I am so ignorant and uncertain in my improvements that I would fain hide my attempts and failures in solitude where they shall perplex none or very few beside myself. The result of our secretest attempts will certainly have as much renown as shall be due to it.

I do not look on myself as a valuable member to any community which is not either very large or very small and select. I fear that your's would not find me as profitable and pleasant an associate as I should wish to be, and as so important a project seems imperatively to require in all its constituents.

Mr. Edmund Hosmer, a very intelligent farmer and a very upright man in my neighborhood, to whom I read your letter, admired the spirit of the plan but distrusted all I told him of the details as far as they concerned the farm.

1. He said, as a general rule nothing was gained by coöperation in a farm, except in those few pieces of work which cannot be done alone, like getting in a load of hay, which takes three men. In every other case, it is better to séparate the workmen. His own boys (all good boys) work better separately than with him.

2. He thought Mr. Ripley should put no dependence on the results of gentlemen farmers such as Mr. P—— and others who were named. If his (Mr. Hosmer's) farm had been managed in the way of Mr. P——'s, it would have put himself and family 'n the poor-house long ago. If Mr. P——'s farm should be exhibited in an accurate account of debt

and credit from his beginning until now, it would probably show a great deficit. Another consideration : The gentlemen farmers are obliged to conduct their operations by means of a foreman whom they choose because he has skill to make ends meet, and sell the produce without any scrupulous inquiry on the part of the employer as to his methods. That foreman buys cheap and sells dear, in a manner which Mr. Ripley and his coadjutors will not sanction. The same thing is true of many farmers, whose praise is in the agricultural reports. If they were honest there would be no brilliant results. And Mr. Hosmer is sure that no large property can ever be made by honest farming.

3. Mr. Hosmer thinks the equal payment of ten cents per hour to every laborer unjust. One man brings capital to the community and receives his interest. He has little skill to labor. A farmer also comes who has no capital but can do twice as much as Mr. Hosmer in a day. His skill is his capital. It would be unjust to pay him no interest on that.

4. Mr. Hosmer disbelieves that good work will continue to be done for the community if the worker is not directly benefited. His boys receive a cent a basket for the potatoes they bring in, and that makes them work, though they know very well that the whole produce of the farm is for them.

INDEX.

———

AMERICAN
COMMONWEALTHS

Volumes devoted to such States of the Union as have a striking political, social, or economic history. Each volume, with Map and Index, 16mo, gilt top, $1.25 *net;* postage extra. The set, 19 vols., $23.75 *net;* half polished morocco, $52.25 *net.*

The books which form this series are scholarly and readable individually; collectively, the series, when completed, will present a history of the nation, setting forth in lucid and vigorous style the varieties of government and of social life to be found in the various commonwealths included in the federal union.

CALIFORNIA. By JOSIAH ROYCE.
CONNECTICUT. By ALEXANDER JOHNSTON. (Revised Ed.)
INDIANA. By J. P. DUNN, JR. (Revised Edition.)
KANSAS. By LEVERETT W. SPRING. (Revised Edition.)
KENTUCKY. By NATHANIEL SOUTHGATE SHALER.
LOUISIANA. By ALBERT PHELPS.
MARYLAND. By WILLIAM HAND BROWNE. (Revised Ed.)
MICHIGAN. By THOMAS M. COOLEY. (Revised Edition.)
MINNESOTA. By WM. W. FOLWELL.
MISSOURI. By LUCIEN CARR.
NEW HAMPSHIRE. By FRANK B. SANBORN.
NEW YORK. By ELLIS H. ROBERTS. 2 vols. (Revised Ed.)
OHIO. By RUFUS KING. (Revised Edition.)
RHODE ISLAND. By IRVING B. RICHMAN.
TEXAS. By GEORGE P. GARRISON.
VERMONT. By ROWLAND E. ROBINSON.
VIRGINIA. By JOHN ESTEN COOKE. (Revised Edition.)
WISCONSIN. By REUBEN GOLD THWAITES.

In preparation

GEORGIA. By ULRICH B. PHILLIPS.
ILLINOIS. By JOHN H. FINLEY.
IOWA. By ALBERT SHAW.
MASSACHUSETTS. By EDWARD CHANNING.
NEW JERSEY. By AUSTIN SCOTT.
OREGON. By F. H. HODDER.
PENNSYLVANIA. By TALCOTT WILLIAMS.

HOUGHTON MIFFLIN COMPANY

AMERICAN STATESMEN

Biographies of Men famous in the Political History of the United States. Edited by JOHN T. MORSE, JR. Each volume, 16mo, gilt top, $1.25 *net*, postage extra. The set, 31 volumes, $38.75 *net;* half morocco, $85.25 *net.*

*Separately they are interesting and entertaining biographies of our most emi-
nent public men ; as a series they are especially remarkable as constituting a
history of American politics and policies more complete and more useful for instruction and reference than any that I am aware of.* — HON. JOHN W. GRIGGS,
Ex-United States Attorney-General.

BENJAMIN FRANKLIN. By JOHN T. MORSE, JR.
SAMUEL ADAMS. By JAMES K. HOSMER.
PATRICK HENRY. By MOSES COIT TYLER.
GEORGE WASHINGTON. By HENRY CABOT LODGE. 2 volumes.
JOHN ADAMS. By JOHN T. MORSE, JR.
ALEXANDER HAMILTON. By HENRY CABOT LODGE.
GOUVERNEUR MORRIS. By THEODORE ROOSEVELT.
JOHN JAY. By GEORGE PELLEW.
JOHN MARSHALL. By ALLAN B. MAGRUDER.
THOMAS JEFFERSON. By JOHN T. MORSE, JR.
JAMES MADISON. By SYDNEY HOWARD GAY.
ALBERT GALLATIN. By JOHN AUSTIN STEVENS.
JAMES MONROE. By D. C. GILMAN.
JOHN QUINCY ADAMS. By JOHN T. MORSE, JR. |
JOHN RANDOLPH. By HENRY ADAMS.
ANDREW JACKSON. By W. G. SUMNER.
MARTIN VAN BUREN. By EDWARD W. SHEPARD.
HENRY CLAY. By CARL SCHURZ. 2 volumes.
DANIEL WEBSTER. By HENRY CABOT LODGE.
JOHN C. CALHOUN. By DR. H. VON HOLST.
THOMAS H. BENTON. By THEODORE ROOSEVELT.
LEWIS CASS. By ANDREW C. MCLAUGHLIN.
ABRAHAM LINCOLN. By JOHN T. MORSE, JR. 2 volumes.
WILLIAM H. SEWARD. By THORNTON K. LOTHROP.
SALMON P. CHASE. By ALBERT BUSHNELL HART.
CHARLES FRANCIS ADAMS. By C. F. ADAMS, JR.
CHARLES SUMNER. By MOORFIELD STOREY.
THADDEUS STEVENS. By SAMUEL W. MCCALL.

SECOND SERIES

Biographies of men particularly influential in the recent Political History of the
Nation. Each volume, with Portrait, 12mo, $1.25 *net ;* postage extra.

*This second series is intended to supplement the original list of American
Statesmen by the addition of the names of men who have helped to make the history of the United States since the Civil War.*

JAMES G. BLAINE. By EDWARD STANWOOD.
JOHN SHERMAN. By THEODORE E. BURTON.
ULYSSES S. GRANT. By SAMUEL W. MCCALL. In preparation.

Other interesting additions to the list to be made in the future.

HOUGHTON MIFFLIN COMPANY

AMERICAN MEN OF LETTERS

WILLIAM CULLEN BRYANT. By JOHN BIGELOW.

J. FENIMORE COOPER. By T. R. LOUNSBURY.

GEORGE WILLIAM CURTIS. By EDWARD CARY.

RALPH WALDO EMERSON. By OLIVER WENDELL HOLMES.

BENJAMIN FRANKLIN. By JOHN BACH MCMASTER.

NATHANIEL HAWTHORNE. By GEORGE E. WOODBERRY.

WASHINGTON IRVING. By CHARLES DUDLEY WARNER.

SIDNEY LANIER. By EDWIN MIMS.

HENRY W. LONGFELLOW. By T. W. HIGGINSON.

JAMES RUSSELL LOWELL. By FERRIS GREENSLET.

MARGARET FULLER OSSOLI. By T. W. HIGGINSON.

FRANCIS PARKMAN. By H. D. SEDGWICK.

EDGAR ALLAN POE. By GEORGE E. WOODBERRY.

WILLIAM HICKLING PRESCOTT. By ROLLO OGDEN.

GEORGE RIPLEY. By O. B. FROTHINGHAM.

WILLIAM GILMORE SIMMS. By WILLIAM P. TRENT.

BAYARD TAYLOR. By ALBERT H. SMYTH.

HENRY D. THOREAU. By FRANK B. SANBORN.

NOAH WEBSTER. By HORACE E. SCUDDER.

WALT WHITMAN. By BLISS PERRY.

JOHN GREENLEAF WHITTIER. By GEO. R. CARPENTER.

NATHANIEL PARKER WILLIS. By HENRY A. BEERS.

The set, 22 volumes, $27.50 *net;* half-polished morocco, $60.50 *net.*

In preparation

BRET HARTE. By HENRY C. MERWIN.

OLIVER WENDELL HOLMES. By S. M. CROTHERS.

Other titles to be added.

HOUGHTON MIFFLIN COMPANY